# THE LIGHT *of* EDEN

D1523396

# THE
# LIGHT *of* EDEN
## *a Christian Worldview*

*by*

# HAROLD C. RALEY

JOHN M. HARDY PUBLISHING
ALPINE & HOUSTON

2008

First Printing: April 2008

ISBN 0-9798391-2-2

Cover Design - Leisha Israel

Cover Art: "Land of Paradise"
by Jan Brueghel the Elder
Courtesy of Veer®

John M. Hardy Publishing
Houston, Texas

www.johnmhardy.com

# THE LIGHT *of* EDEN

# TABLE OF CONTENTS

# FOREWORD

From time to time I come across a book that captures my imagination and expands my vision. On those rare occasions, I find myself thinking, "I wish I had thought of that" or "I wish I had written that." This kind of writer's envy is the occupational hazard of many people who lecture and write. Harold Raley's *The Light of Eden* is the sort of book I wish I had written.

But even in less humble moments, I have no illusions that I could have written this particular book. It is the product of a unique man and exceptional mind. From the Prologue to the Epilogue readers will find themselves taken into Raley's philosophical tale. The book is refreshing, insightful, mature and at times a bit frightening. It is not an ordinary book in any way.

Harold Raley's project in these pages is ambitious. He wants nothing less than to construct and promote a distinctively Christian worldview, a comprehensive approach to life with all its complexities and ambiguities. Faith here is not some life option which you can take or leave at will. Spirituality is not an amorphous feel-good program, a one-size-fits-all system of positive thinking or self-realization. In Raley's vision of the Christian life there is no simple dichotomy between the secular and the sacred. As he writes, he challenges and deconstructs the facile façade the West has built under the banner of Christ. With the patience and skill of an artist Raley reveals how Western Christian culture has failed to live up to the magnificent philosophical, intellectual, political, ethical, and theological traditions we have inherited from the ancients. He mines the canon of literature to sculpt a worldview completely consonant with the audacious claims of the Christian faith and frequently at odds with the cowardly conduct evident in much of the Christian West.

If there is a scandalous lack of evangelical minds, as Mark Noll has lamented, he did not have Harold Raley in mind. These are the mature reflections of a gentle and pleasant man, formed in quiet piety and fashioned by years of academic study and teaching. He proffers all who venture on the journey a brilliant and compelling image of the life of faith. Every sentence is skillfully crafted, aesthetically pleasing and philosophically challenging. At times his lofty prose feels more like poetry. There is never a wasted word.

Fortunately for us, Harold Raley has not been infected by the pandemic of political correctness. Like a big league umpire, he calls them as he sees them. Unlike other social commentators, he refuses to worship the idol of broadmindedness. In fact, he argues persuasively that many modern values will become our undoing unless they are tempered with the kind of moral and spiritual excellence the West has left behind.

Raley invites us into his own personal pilgrimage toward excellence, an excellence of heart, mind, strength, and thought. But in sharing his journey with us, Raley makes it possible for all of us to experience afresh "the Light of Eden."

David B. Capes, Ph.D.
Chair of Christianity and Philosophy
Houston Baptist University

# PROLOGUE

Billboards and bumper stickers tell us that Christ is the answer, but in truth he is something infinitely greater: the Light of the World that shines in the darkness, illuminating the way to our own answers and a deeper understanding of our problems. Since Eden the divine light has shone across the human ages with varying magnitude, dimly in the times of mankind's falling away from truth, brightly in the years of its recovery, brilliantly when Christ walked the earth. Often shadowed but never overshadowed, the Light of Eden is forever obedient to God's first command in *Genesis*: there shall be light and it shall be separate from the darkness.

✝✝✝

This book is about dimensions of human life best understood under this divine illumination. Or so I believe. From this standpoint I shall suggest new or amended ways of understanding personhood, sexuate life, society, aesthetics, history, nature, the Bible, the Church, and Christian destiny, along with tempting detours into topics too many to count here. The neologism "sexuate" refers to the human traits, including sexuality, that differentiate us as men and women. I shall touch on these distinctions in a later chapter.

When carried to their full implications, the dimensions, problems, and levels of life discussed in this book form what I understand to be a Christian worldview. With many gaps and probable blind spots in my understanding, I should add.

None of these themes, and none of their drama, is detached from my own life, for this book is also the story of my journey from philosophical skepticism to faith. I write what I have lived. My conversion began as a tiny circumscribed fire within my skeptical spirit, but sparks jumped the defenses set up to contain its spread, and simmering long years unseen, eventually blazed forth to engulf everything in its way. No part of my life was spared its consuming flame. Too late to save my old secular paradigm, I learned that one does not trifle with the Divine. God is dangerously good.

Consumed but still unconvinced, I surveyed my old life in an aftermath of spiritual topsy-turvy and intellectual dismay. The wreckage embarrassed and pained me in equal measure. I resented the suffering it caused me, more so because it came at an age when most of my family and friends had long since settled their religious accounts. Later, however, I began to see that what we are unwilling to suffer we are unable to enjoy, and that to avoid suffering is to evade maturity. But at the time such notions were heretical to my Protestant understanding, as evident as they were unacceptable.

Time and truth had their way, however, and eventually I had to bid goodbye to many fond things, for what I had known, or thought I knew, archived in old intellectual hierarchies, had now become inconsistencies in the way I had lived and believed. Long convicted and finally convinced, I ran no further, but turning, embraced the truth that had first embraced me. And as my old, skeptical understanding of the Christian life crumbled into ashes, a richer and more hopeful perspective opened before me. This book is about that vision.

None of the themes in this book will be exhaustively treated. Think of them as dots that one may connect to form a coherent image or road signs to guide the traveler. The earnest seeker of truth, the willing student, the devoted disciple, does not need to be led by the hand to his destination. It is enough to point him sympathetically in the right direction. True learning and truthful living occurs as he goes the rest of the way on his own. If my story offers any comfort to my traveling companions, it will be as an encour-

aging word, a helping hand, a shared fellowship in
Christian Truth.

I cannot now, as once I could, fix a boundary between the
sacred and the secular. It is altogether fitting to revere most
what is foremost to God. We concede him Church, and
Creed, and Kingdom, but we have it on good authority that
he also holds dear the daintiest flower of the field and
attends the decease of the loneliest sparrow. No earnest
believer would disagree, but this pious acknowledgment of
the universal sovereignty of God is easier made than
handily managed in the devilish details of everyday life.

The clamor of our time is a general blasphemy against the
degraded state of the world. Everyone, it seems, is sick to
death of modernity. Not that we must read tomes and treatises to understand our plight. The great human dilemmas
cry out in our heart before they shout in our headlines.
Nothing is a problem until it becomes personal.

We have made a mantra of post-modernism, claiming by
rote what has yet to be confirmed by reason. In this generalized disgust there lies a hidden paradox of history. No age
has had more means or enjoyed more comforts than modernity, yet none has produced grimmer philosophies or lived
more fearfully. Someday it will surely be said of modern
man that for dread of dying he dared not live. (Though
sensitive to gender problems in English usage, I prefer the
term "man" in its old Germanic sense of "one," i.e., a person
of either sex.)

On the other hand, we also confront a mystery: how was
it that the Middle Ages, dismissed by many moderns as dull
and dark, created positive philosophies and showed a
grand zest for life? I shall take up this theme again in
another context.

Today we long to bury modernity and dance on its grave.
But to step ahead of our story, we must do more than celebrate as fact what may yet be only fable. For the highest
authority has told us that until we discover the Kingdom of
God within us, the failings of this "broken world," this
*monde cassé*, as Christian philosopher Gabriel Marcel

describes it, will continue to be the stuff and nonsense of our life. Otherwise, even as we plan a gleeful wake for the modern age its unhappy shade reincarnates under another name.

In fairness, though, we have no right to blame our frustrations on modernity or fault it for its failures. After all, the Modern Age kept its promise to give men the run of this world, asking as an earnest their pledge of faith in the next. The bargain was willingly struck, and only now do we begin to see how shabby the swap.

Most post-Modernists assume as a given that the next age will also be post-Christian. They foresee a time when Christianity will have ceased to be, and it will no longer be necessary for its enemies to be anti-Christian as they are today. The supposition deserves our honest attention. For though our answer may ring with a better hope, we must also ask, is it possible to be Christian after the modern experience? Do we know too much to believe? Or too little? Have facts gained the upper hand over our faith? To be Christian must we live in willful blindness, as our enemies claim, closing our eyes to inconvenient truths? Has the truth of this world trumped the Truth of God?

With other aims in mind, psychologist William James once noted that we listen mostly to those who dwell on the gigantic problems of the world and suggested that now and then we would do well to turn to those who have begun to offer modest answers. His advice was sound, and I shall heed it in this book. Yet I do not quarrel with those who say the world is done for. The world is always done for, always desperate, always at a dead end. And a good thing, too, otherwise it would be too seductive for us to bother ourselves about a fate beyond this life. An all-sufficient earthly life was the dream of modernity, and also its debacle. Modern secularists lived down a lesser ideal, while Christians failed to live up to a greater one. But that means that the promise born into this world as Christ remains intact, ever able to spring to life again in a golden age of faith. Christianity is all about rebirth.

In my meditations on the shape this book might take, I had to make a prior decision. I could choose either the easier task of developing a few concepts or the riskier way of presenting a much wider panorama of problems and possibilities inherent in Christianity. I chose the latter not only because it partially reflected the totality of my conversion experience but also because I had hopes that others more gifted than I could mold my bare notions into usable forms. I still hope so. And I wanted to offer them while their revelation was still fresh. Truth is strongest when it erupts in our life as the illuminating moment of truth, what the Greeks called *alétheia* and Christians would describe as *apocalypse*. After the moment has passed, even the most extraordinary revelations settle into the routine levels of life, there to be domesticated as dogma and archived as fact.

As a consequence of this choice, it is not my intention to write a "deep" book. Quite the opposite; because it has a philosophical dimension, this is, or so I hope, a superficial writing. I must explain why. Things are shy and like to hide their reality in depth and darkness, and every reluctant revelation becomes in turn a condition of their further concealment. It is not the thinker's duty to connive with them in their elusiveness by covering them with opaque thoughts but to coax them out of the darkness into the light. Clarity is the courtesy a writer offers the reader, but this age has warred against good manners, and literary civility is among the casualties. In a friendlier sense, true philosophy is the general art of superficiality, the art of bringing hidden things to the surface where we can see and understand them with ordinary intelligence. Mistaking depth for intelligence and ignoring the greatest legacy of the Enlightenment, the Modern Age became obsessed with deep thinking, and as a consequence much of what it produced turned out to be an unintentional conspiracy to keep things in concealment and readers in the dark.

I make this process sound more straightforward than it was. The vague outline of this book began to obsess me nearly twenty years before I started to write it. Three factors

delayed me: the first was that I believed others better quali-
fied than I should write it. Once I suggested it to a
prominent Catholic philosopher, but he shook his head and
said that since I had the idea it probably meant the task was
mine. I explained that I was not Catholic. He smiled and
advised me to wait.

The second and simplest reason for my delay was that it
took me a long time to shape and refine the ideas themselves. A couple of failed early attempts convinced me that
I could take no shortcuts, and that despite my impatience I
had no choice but to wait, serving in the meantime a lengthy
apprenticeship of teaching, studying, writing, and medi-
tating on the Bible, history, philosophy, literature, religion,
art, and language.

The third reason was even more critical: I had to find the
right literary style and tone for the writing, as a musician
must find the right key before playing. Far from being an
incidental peculiarity of writing, the style of a work is an
inseparable part of its reality. Buffon wrote that style is the
man. For better or worse and in ways I could by no means
explain, the style that finally emerged is the transmuted life
I have lived and the man I have become.

Understood in this expanded sense, style is the road to
originality. But this statement must be rightly interpreted.
The modern mania for "originality" has resulted in a clutter
of unoriginal art, music, thought, and behavior. Poetry, for
instance, is the moribund victim of this collective frenzy.
The Modern Age never quite learned to distinguish
between originality and outlandishness, just as it assumed
that meaningful being could only mean being different.
Many generations of artists, writers, and reformers were
victimized in their art and in their lives by this skewed
philosophy.

Now we begin to see things a bit more clearly. To go to
extremes to be different from everybody else is simply to
run in step with a herd of similar extremists. When everybody dissents, dissension becomes conformity. In another
context C. S. Lewis once said that whereas the saints are

truly original, the despots of history are predictably similar. And Goethe summarized the reason when he wrote that when men turn from the Creator they soon cease to be creative. A positive but blander version of the rule applies to us all: true originality happens when we are true to our origins.

Duly alerted by my own remarks, I shall not set out deliberately to be original in this book but instead faithful and responsible to the truth as I see it. The originality, if any, of what I have to say will have to take care of itself. In that candid spirit, I must say that most of what I shall present incorporates my rethought renderings of things learned from a host of sources too vast to call by name or title. My debts lie prolific in all directions: books, preachers, priests, philosophers, theologians, teachers, students, mentors, friends, colleagues, novelists, poets, family, children, and those whom the world incorrectly calls common people.

And of a higher order and category all its own, the Bible.

# I

## BIBLICAL PERSPECTIVES

What are we to make of the Bible? Thomas Paine wrote that because of the cruelties, debaucheries, and executions that fill half its pages it resembles more the harmful word of a demon than the benign revelation of God. But William Blake cautions the Bible-haters:

> *And better had they ne'er been born,*
> *Who read to doubt, or read to scorn.*

I raise the question in this preliminary context; the rest of the book will be my way of responding to it.

✝ ✝ ✝

### 1. The Bible: A Personal Encounter

I ended the Prologue by saying that as an influence on my way of thinking the Bible was in a category all its own. But I must not give the impression that its impact was continuous, at least not consciously continuous. Some projects, like some people, cross the far corners of our life and disappear from view, barely leaving a trace. Others busy us for a season then sink into the subterranean depths of our being only to resurface many years later with unresolved claims on us. What truly calls us in the beginning always requires of us a moral accounting in the end. And this final reckoning casts a defining sheen of fulfillment or failure over our lives.

So it is now with me: seemingly quiescent for many

years, the Bible has returned to strike the original tone and take the late measure of my life, for much of my story flows also through its pages. The world may lead us far from our earliest ideals, but if we walk in truth, the further we go the nearer we come to them again, perhaps to rescue them with a greater benevolence, perhaps to love them again as though for the first time.

The Bible was foundational in my life and my way of thinking, which is why I struggled so mightily against it as a young intellectual. In the lower Appalachian land of my youth the Scriptures were as solid as the ground we stood on and as unquestioned as the air we breathed. Passionately preached in our "full-gospel" churches—none claimed to be anything more or less—often sincerely misconstrued, many times ignored yet always morally absolute, the Bible was at once a comfort and a caution, switching in a twinkling in our hands from heavenly promise to hellish perdition. It was as familiar as our hills and valleys yet replete with images of distant lands and alien ways. It was our Bible but it told of other flocks we knew not of. We changed the names and the story became ours, yet unbeknownst to us it was sowing in our spirits the seeds of higher understanding and deeper compassion. In our backcountry we were hard in our hatreds and harsh in our vices yet ever liable to commit good deeds and lead better lives because of the Word's divine subversion.

In the beginning the Bible was a book to read; later it would become a universe to explore. It was old before it was new to me. It was a paradox and a perplexity. I was disturbed by passages I could not understand and, like Mark Twain, distressed by many that I could. Its narrative rhythm was oddly syncopated: at times it said too little and at others, too much, and seemingly in the wrong way. It was casual with logic yet gave signs of a greater reason than I knew.

The Bible served us as the lower court of divine judgment. By its truths, never doubted, ever debated, our hardened sinners knew they were betting their soul against eternity. Obsessed with these everlasting issues, our preachers barely acknowledged the minor wrongs that trouble softer Christians. Nor were they skilled in the symbolic transfers that democratize wickedness and from the sins of one make equal sinners of us all. There was no corporate sin-sharing; society assumed none of our personal guilt. For us the absolutes still held, and the center was solid; the boundaries traced of old between good and evil were seldom redrawn and never withdrawn. Our transgressions were mirthless and mighty, for only the grimmest sins could stand against the biblical warnings that pressured them relentlessly. With inverse admiration we marveled at the misplaced courage of our great sinners, celebrated their repentance, and grieved for them when they lost their wager with death. And though within the faithful fold ourselves, we struggled with the mystifying language and hard mysteries of the Bible, and as unable to understand them as we were ready to defend them, declared all the more our fearful reverence for the Great Author of our confusion.

Part of the problem, a major part as I came to see later, was that the words of the Bible were all we had and, so we proudly proclaimed, all we needed. Yet in time I came to understand that a book is not just what is written on its pages but also the silent suppositions that surround it like a halo and complete its meanings. Most books are half written between the lines or off the pages; many things need not be explained or narrated textually because everybody knows them contextually. Probably we miss essential implications in what Plato, or Aristotle, or Moses wrote because we are unaware of the buzzing gossip in the Athenian Areopagus or the cant and carping of the wandering Hebrews in the desert. Every book is first of all a dialogue with its circumstantial world, and insofar as we miss the prompts and protocols of the exchange our understanding is diminished.

After many centuries the Bible reached us half a world away from its origins, but its enlightening cultural and literary context was lost along the way. Lacking this extra-textual cohort we added our own, and this odd combination of ancient text and improvised context created a new book. If the words of the Bible were universally inerrant, as we wholeheartedly believed, the context was locally circumstanced. As a result, the message we read probably was not quite the same message that was written. The Bible may not have been meant for us, but we insisted that we were meant for it, and we added our meanings accordingly.

The result was that despite its genuine fervor and godly intentions, our Christianity sometimes veered close to a kind of "bibliolatry." In our lust for Heaven we were apt to subsume the God of Abraham, Isaac, and Jacob in our reverence for the Bible and make him a prisoner of the Book.

Yet if Heaven was our priority, this world was our preference. We proclaimed that we were living in the last days yet prayed that our days would last. We feared Hell and dreaded Heaven. All was stark and straightforward, and nothing mitigated. We spoke ill of this life yet cherished every minute of it. Our Christianity promised everlasting life yet grieved us with stigmas of death, hell, and the grave. Our faith made exiles of us all: we were here but not from here. Life to us was not the triumphant march of the world's winners but the painful pilgrimage of its wounded. In matters of religion we were sympathetic to the illiterate and suspicious of the educated, and if at times our elders spoke favorably of learning, they had in mind a salary, not our salvation. We revered the first Christians and suspected heresy in everything since. And we were determined that our faith would remain always a theological infant never to grow beyond its primal beginnings.

In the universities I came to know other orthodoxies and their own internal heresies. The Hebrews and their Judeo-Christian successors had taught me to worship; now from the Greeks and their philosophic descendants I learned something of the life of the mind. After undergoing the normal rituals of intellectual seduction and sophomoric skepticism about my rural biblical tradition, I regained enough balance to see that in all things good and lovely and true in our Western civilization we are yet apprentices to our first masters. The twin streams from which we drink converged but never fully merged. We are still Greeks in mind and Hebrews in spirit.

Instead of lamenting this duality as a cultural liability, however, in time I came to see in it a cause for celebration. For in those lands where the curious Greeks did not leave their mark, pure intellectual curiosity did not take root, or at least did not thrive. There, we find no great universities where students pursue knowledge for its own sake. There, mere enchantment with reality itself is rare and learning seldom rises above parochial and utilitarian purposes. This is why one usually has to go to the Hellenized West to learn about the non-Hellenized portions of the world.

† **†** †

## 2. The Bible, Myth, and Human History

Apart from its theological content and promises of redemption, what can we learn from the Bible? To our ancestors the very question would have reeked of heresy. For the answer would have been everything, at least everything worth knowing. For our medieval ancestors the Bible was an abbreviated encyclopedia of human knowledge, an accurate and inerrant narration of the creation, history, and purpose of the world and its people. This belief has not died, certainly not amongst fundamentalist Christians, but it has been challenged and ridiculed within and without Christianity.

"Bible Christians" tenaciously defend biblical infallibility and inerrancy. But to defend something is, by definition, to be defensive and aware that what one defends is imperiled.

There is a vast difference between the unchallenged assurance of earlier Christians and the defensive posture of Bible believers today. Their very vehemence reveals a fear, not so much that they could be wrong about the Bible but that their antagonists may be right. For the Bible-believer there is a flood of hateful truths in the world. In the modern centuries this rising tide has appeared to sweep away one bastion of biblical certainty after another. At each fallback outpost the defense resumes tenacious but the drift is discouraging. Could the unthinkable happen? Is the battle to defend the Bible and the Christian faith about to be lost? In this uncertain context, I repeat the question, what can we learn from the Bible?

To begin, we can consider what our ancestors learned from its pages. The Bible presents a historical and geographical panorama so vast that even if there were no extra-biblical sources to corroborate the information—and in some cases there are none—from its pages alone they learned about Hebrews, Egyptians, Chaldeans, Medes, Persians, Syrians, Cretans, Hittites, Philistines, Canaanites, Arameans, Assyrians, Ethiopians, Romans, Greeks, Amorites, Arabs, Ishmaelites, Midianites, Samaritans, Moabites, Ammonites, and briefer hints of other tribes and peoples. Likewise, they learned about many cities of the ancient world, along with rivers, mountains, seas, lakes, oases, wells, plants, animals, foods, farming, herding, clothing, laws, transportation, religions, heresies, personalities, governance, institutions, monarchs, prophets, gods, customs, vocations, diseases, famines, genealogies, migrations, languages, crimes, tortures, weapons, wars, persecutions, and calamities. The Bible preserves a record of all this and more, including references to the lost world before the Flood and the first human generations. As we shall see, Christianity is the heir to all this and more. But there is more, and this is where the unexplored dimensions of the Bible commence.

Nearly every culture we know of has a creation myth, a mythology about human origins. Most of them involve animals, giants, or elementary forces of nature. Northern Germanic peoples believed that the sweat of the giant Ymir, who was formed from melting ice, gave birth to a man and a woman, the progenitors of the human race. Some Native American tribes, including such disparate groups as the Alabama-Coushatta and the Mexica-Aztecs, for instance, tell how their first ancestors emerged from caves. Many early peoples believed they were descended from animals with which they preserved a special totemic kinship, while the royal families of Egypt, Japan, and Peru claimed to be children of the sun.

Modern anthropologists take these mythologies very seriously, possibly in some cases more so than the people who created and preserved them. In the *Comentarios reales* (Royal Commentaries) of the Peruvian Garcilaso de la Vega (called the "Inca" to distinguish him from his relative, the more famous Spanish poet by the same name), there is a hint that the first Incas, a brother and sister, purposely created, or at least enhanced, the myth of their solar ancestry to bedazzle local clans and bring them into subjugation. Their strategy worked, and the Incan empire spread over a vast territory, for as the neighboring peoples reasoned, the sun was surely more powerful than their own tribal gods.

In *The Everlasting Man* G. K. Chesterton recommends, very wisely it seems to me, that as far as any objective or factual information is concerned we take these fanciful mythologies with a grain of salt. He suggests that they resemble the fictional tales adults create to entertain themselves and their children, knowing all the while that there is a more serious adult explanation of what really happened. The mythologies are "true" only if we suspend ordinary belief and time and accept the rules of the game.

In this regard myth and magic have certain parallels. Magic or shamanism is real for all primitive people we know of, and as vestigial superstitions perhaps for us all. Yet as anthropologist Bronislaw Malinowski reminds us in his classic work *Magic, Science and Religion*, they are not so naïve as to think that magic can be invoked to make a boat or cook a meal. Magic has its place and function in primitive societies, and primitives know its categorical limits, even if ethnologists sometimes do not.

A timelessness hovers about all mythology. Zeus and his cohort of gods were no closer to the Greeks of Plato's day than they are to us. And the same is true of other pantheons. Mythology exists in an absolute past beyond time and history, and even if, as some suspect, certain ancient heroes or rulers—Gilgamesh, Quetzalcoatl, Woden—were originally men apotheosized over time for their exploits, they were also lifted out of time altogether. The gods on Mount Olympus may have once dwelt on earth in real time, but now they live by the Greek Calends.

Unlike practically every other culture, the ancient Hebrews had little or no mythology—unless, as skeptics claim, the Bible itself is a vast mythology. Intellectual honesty requires that we consider the stupendous possibility that the authors of the Bible preserved memories of humanity's earliest experiences. If true, how was it possible for a people of no great numbers or material means to deviate from all others, even those closely related to them? Could they, as they claim, have been divinely chosen for the task of preserving the true message of God and the real story of mankind? How else can we explain their uniqueness?

Although Christians revere the Scriptures, most will candidly agree that the accounts of begetting offspring are its dreariest and most unrewarding passages. We grant them at most a certain importance in fixing later Jewish genealogy, and some Christians, taking their cue from Archbishop Ussher, use them to make calculations about the age of the earth. Otherwise, they seem to have little theological or homiletic capital. But we may have overlooked something too important to pass over. Indeed, far from being the dullest, the "begetting" passages may be among the most important in the Bible. Let me explain why.

These generational series with names, life spans, and

occasional biographical commentary link the biblical account of human origins to historical peoples and circumstances and prevent it from slipping into the timeless mode of mythology. Because of the names the biblical account is anchored in human history. Beginning with the divine creation of the world, an unbroken, unfolding skein of life continues to this very day. As though to remind us anew of this historical link to the creation of mankind, with the birth of Christ the generational series was recapitulated in different versions in the New Testament Gospels of Matthew and Luke. More than Jewish genealogy, which was crucial in establishing the prophetic advent of Jesus as the Messiah, the generational series also implies an anthropological vision of all humanity that I shall explore later.

But there is more. The generational series of both the Old and New Testaments are a further reminder that although God "rested" from his labors on the seventh, or Sabbath, day, divine creation continued as procreation, or "co-creation." This involves unfathomable mysteries but also at least one immediate certainty: from a Christian understanding, human sexuality ought never to be thought of as amusement or mere breeding. Sex involves the sacred mystery of life itself and, as every true lover knows, or discovers, deserves to be entered into with a special kind of purity and reverence.

On the other hand, it is a risky business to align these "begetting" passages in linear chronology and by doing so to impose on the Bible a calendric grid for which it was never intended. Bible scholars suggest that in some cases untold numbers of generations were telescoped under a single eponymous ancestor; otherwise the arithmetical calculations lead to strange paradoxes. By simple linear addition Adam would have died only a hundred twenty-six years before the birth of Noah, and by generational count Noah himself would have lived past the birth of Isaac! By this simple generational count, Eber, the eponymous ancestor of the Hebrews, outlived his descendant Abraham but barely survived Noah himself. Yet it beggars belief to realize that none of their descendants visit or even mention their ancient but presumably still living ancestors. At the same time, there are intriguing consistencies as well. According to the generational arithmetic both Methuselah and his son Lamech perished the year of the Flood, presumably by drowning.

As biblical scholars remind us, in keeping with Semitic practices of the Near East, references to the "father" or sire of certain descendants may indicate the grandfather, great-grandfather, or earlier ancestor. Also the Near Eastern custom of levirate marriage in ancient times, of fathering children in the name of a deceased brother, further complicates, perhaps inextricably so, what appeared to Archbishop Ussher and others to be a straightforward matter of arithmetic calculation in the sequential Western mode. In chronology document 4Q559, known as "Calendrical Scrolls," of *The Dead Sea Scrolls Uncovered* by Robert Eisenman and Michael Wise we find this enigmatic reference: (The total of) all these [years:] ". . . eleven thousand, five hundred and thirty-six. . . ." The authors explain that at the time of the Qumran community there were at least three separate systems for calculating biblical chronology, none of them in accord with Archbishop Ussher's method.

✝✝✝

### 3. A Reasoning from Silence: The Early Years of Jesus

Theologians warn us against arguing from silence, especially where the Bible is concerned. But judging from tortured interpretations of extant biblical documents, reasoning from canonical sources is hardly more certain or less risky. The old Protestant rule, "speak where the Bible speaks and be silent where the Bible is silent," may appear to settle the argument in favor of prudence and common sense, but what is approved in theory has never been applied in fact. Probably nothing in the history of Christianity has been debated more divisively than the biblical "silences" and what to do about them. Almost from the beginnings of Christianity, and more acutely since the advent of Protestantism, theologians have insisted on shedding light where human light cannot go. Often the greater problem is not what the Bible says but what it does not say. Why should this be? Why despite our precautions and better judgment are we compelled to argue about the silences of the Bible?

I considered what could be called the "contextual or extra-textual presupposition of silence" in Chapter 1. But there are other kinds of silence. Under a single name it can be eloquent and golden or cowardly and conniving. There are selfish silences like forbidding deserts that offer nothing to our soul, but others are watered oases which yearn for our arrival like an awaited advent and offer us room for a spiritual colonization. We read that in the beginning God spoke, and from his Word, from the *Logos*, in the primal silence of eternity past, worlds and galaxies, creatures and men came into being. Theologians are fond of saying that God created the world out of nothingness, *ex-nihilo*. But is this not a misplaced fondness? For the Word was anything but nothingness. In it, in him, were contained—are contained—all the possibilities of mankind and the cosmos. Human history is the record of the continuing, creative Word. Yielding to its expanding power, the primeval silence gives way to creations of music, art, mathematics, poetry, and worship, to the concepts of law, ethics, science, theology, and philosophy, to the forms of understanding, to the multiplicities of love.

Here mankind enters into collaboration with creation. We were not born for silence but for the Word. Even in the common course of life taciturnity is a much exaggerated virtue. It is our destiny and our duty to verbalize creation; to the primeval creation we add ideal planes of reality by word and art and song. Nothing is fully understandable until we can utter it. No wonder, then, that Adam's first task was to name the creatures of Eden. This is why anything human must be told in order to be understood. Ours is a narrative reality.

But how can we tell a story when all we have is silence, when our sources are too sparse to support a narration? A case to illustrate the point and make observations is the so-called "silent years" of Jesus.

Someone, perhaps Georges Sand, once said that good women have no story, which also means, by analogy, that neither do good men. In both cases, the thinking is not only wrong but wrongheaded as well. The greatest story ever told was about supreme goodness. Probably we pay too much attention to scoundrels, including repentant scoundrels. The greater their offenses the more their contrition impresses us. But if we are honest about it, we are likely to find a prurient element in our sympathy. Nothing fascinates us so much as to peer into the pit where others fell and to congratulate ourselves self-righteously that we did not.

It is good, of course, to celebrate a rascal's change of heart, but we would do well—and perhaps better—to pay more heed to those who did not first stumble in darkness before seeing the light. Great sinners' dramatic stories of repentance plant in the minds of the gullible—in other words, everybody—the impression that immorality is an acceptable prelude to right living. Young artists and writers, for instance, often make the mistaken determination to indulge in the riotous life in the skewed assumption that they need life experience in order to create works to benefit humanity. It is then easy to persuade oneself that a liberal dose of early sinfulness is a condition of mature virtue. But this happens only in exceptional cases; many people spend their early life preparing miseries that will sully their later years.

The canonical Gospels give us very little factual information about the first thirty years of Jesus' life. We learn about the peculiar problems his birth posed for Mary and Joseph, the birth scene in Bethlehem, the visit by the Magi or Wise Men, the prophecies by Simeon and Anna concerning the infant Jesus, the attempts by Herod to murder the Christ child, the flight to Egypt to save his life, and after Herod's death the family's return to a village called Nazareth in Galilee. But as for the rest of his childhood, adolescence, and early adulthood, we have only the episode of twelve-year-old Jesus in the Temple, his only recorded words before beginning his public ministry, and finally the gospel writer's brief summation of those years: "And the child grew, and waxed strong in spirit, filled with wisdom; and the grace of God was upon him" (*St. Luke* 2:40).

We must not mistake this lack of documentation for the absence of a story. Documented history is fall fruit, the ripe maturity that follows youthful growth. We know much about the declining ages of Greece and Rome, much less about their youthful growth. Young cultures make history; old cultures write it. And so it was with Christianity in the beginning.

These "lost years" have led to much speculation, including spurious biographical material created to fill in the gaps: supposed studies in Tibet, India, or Egypt, a childhood of miraculous—and sometimes malicious—pranks, run-ins with his teacher, etc. But in the absence of reliable canonical records, our only biographical alternative is to comment on the silence itself, on what was *not* said about Jesus. Silence can be golden; in the case of Jesus it may also be eloquently revealing.

As a preliminary, consider first what was said as a response to his worried but relieved parents upon locating him in the Temple: "How is it that ye sought me? Know ye not that I must be about my Father's business?" (*St. Luke* 2:49). Apparently, Jesus did not consider himself lost but already centered in what his life was about. Unless we take them to be the remarks of a thoughtless, headstrong child, his answer to the question any anguished mother would ask presupposes that his parents were, or ought to have been, aware of his special status and mission. In a manner of speaking, it was they who had strayed from his mission. Of his clear foreknowledge of who he was and what he was to do the context hardly leaves any doubt.

Who remembered and reported this incident? The later public activities of Jesus as recorded in the four Gospels were written down by the various apostles, their close assistants, and perhaps other eyewitnesses. But probably they would have known little or nothing about his childhood or adolescence, and there is little documented indication that Jesus himself took time to speak of his childhood.

We may reasonably assume that the childhood information came from his mother and kinfolk. A tradition has come down to us that physician Luke, who may also have been an artist, grew close to the Virgin Mary and that he painted the first Madonna and Child scene. The episode in the Temple is an experience no parent would forget. In the same context we read that Mary "…kept all these sayings in her heart" (*St. Luke*, 2:51).

But we are left to wonder why Luke did not record other sayings and deeds of the young Jesus. There are several possible reasons for the silence. First, it may have been because Mary herself chose not to reveal more information, that indeed she kept these things in her heart or, second, that there were no other extraordinary episodes to tell. For his part, it is hardly likely that the meticulously thorough Luke would not have recorded known facts about Jesus. As he says at the beginning of his gospel, not only did he have the advantage of many sources and the reports of eyewitnesses but also wished to share this knowledge with his unidentified friend Theophilus (*St. Luke* 1:3-4).

With predictable regularity and embarrassing failure over the ages, false prophets have predicted the Second Coming. Christianity has always been a religion of the expectant—and the impatient. Even the first followers of Christ, including the Apostles, believed he would return shortly, probably within their own lifetime. Hence there was no perceived need of historical documentation.

Scholars tell us that only as the first generations of believers began to die off did a need for written testimony arise. Many generations—indeed many centuries—would pass before the written accounts of the Gospel came to be esteemed more highly by some Christians than the oral traditions passed down from eyewitnesses.

The last verse of *St. Luke* 2 tells us that Jesus conformed in every way to what was expected of him. We should not be surprised, for as Jesus would teach later, he came not to abolish the Law but to fulfill it. Obedience, not rebelliousness, characterized his whole life.

What does this mean? In the first place, it implies that by conforming fully to the Law he lived in strict obedience to his parents. Had he been given to unlawful or unruly behavior, he could not have found favor in the eyes of God and men and, further, would have failed from the start in his messianic mission. Even though aware of shortcomings and expediencies that had worked their way into the Law to accommodate imperfect men—in matters of divorce, for example—and the veniality of a great many priests, Jesus nevertheless prepared himself for his great work by honoring, not violating the Mosaic teachings. To repeat at a much higher level a principle introduced earlier, his originality arose not from repudiating the Law but by first obeying it and then innovating within it, thus bringing it to a brilliant fulfillment. He was original by being true to his Jewish origins. The Law was God's Law and Jesus was obedient to God in all things.

We would show poor discernment indeed to mistake the moral purity and submission to authority we find in Jesus for mediocrity of spirit or blandness of character. Though a common expectation, moral purity is never a commonplace virtue but a high form of intelligence and a mastery of self, and of those to whom great authority is given, great obedience is required.

Even though the Bible is equally silent about earlier supernatural works, we can reasonably assume that the Cana miracle was not his first. It is unthinkable that Mary would have risked embarrassing her son publicly by asking of him something he was incapable of doing. She appeared to have no doubt at all that Jesus not only would do what she asked of him but also that he could do it. We can only surmise that she had seen similar miracles, just as we can deduce from the story that Jesus and his mother were very close to each other.

These are plausible reasons why we have little "news" about the young Jesus. Probably, his life was not a series of anomalies and misdeeds, the usual content of "news" as we know it today. On the contrary, it is reasonable to think that he led a normal life, perhaps it would be better to say, an extraordinarily normal life, and it was in this solid, reverent environment that he nurtured the power and wisdom to perform the extraordinary acts that characterized his later ministry. It is much the same for every person but of course not on the same scale or to the same degree. Our early life is absorbent, a gathering of virtues—or vices—from which later acts will flow. Jesus seems to have given few public signs of the greatness that was gestating within his spirit. For this reason, his neighbors were unwilling to concede him the status of a prophet. "Is this not the carpenter's son ...?" Often, the people we know best are also the ones we know least.

How, then, do we penetrate into the biographical life of a person, especially a divine person, whose biography offers only scant facts? There exists a phenomenon, which I call the "sympathy of circumstances," that allows us to transmigrate to the lives of people far from us in culture and time. Without this sympathetic bond every human life, even those closest to us, would be an impenetrable mystery; and understanding biography, fiction, and history would become impossibilities.

But is this bond possible in the case of Jesus? Dare we think as mere mortals that we can establish such a sympathetic bond with Christ? Are we able on any level to understand his life? We do not know specifically the things that happened to him, but from the information available to us we can have a reasonable idea of how he would have "happened" to things. St. Paul writes that we are to have the mind of Christ (*Phil.* 2:5-11). This means that we can know his character, and as the Greeks taught, character is destiny. We worship Christ in his divinity; we understand him in his humanity, that is, in his biographical story which we know as the Gospel.

It is reasonable to think this sympathetic biographical resonance is more possible with Christ than with anyone else. The divinity of Jesus does not lessen the person he is but enhances it instead, and by doing so, enhances our understanding. It is the darkened, sinful, inhuman portions of human personality—in ourselves and others—that block our sympathies and hinder our understanding. Sin separates and obscures; love unites and sheds light.

If at times it seems that we cannot see the forest for the trees, it is much more likely in our day that we cannot tell the story for the facts. Regardless of how much information we have about another life, the sympathetic transmigration I speak of happens only when we bring our imagination into play. Without it we trip on the facts and miss the truth. For imagination is not the enemy of truth as we may think but its complement. The poet Antonio Machado wrote, very insightfully it seems to me, that "...truth is also a creation."

It is important here to distinguish between imagination and mere fantasy or daydreaming, which to our confusion often pass for imagination. The stage on which imagination acts for our greatest benefit is concrete reality, including human reality. Its work is not easy as we may first think, for nothing is harder to imagine than reality itself. The supreme test of imagination is the attempt to enter another life, to connect the random facts and recreate the vital world of that person.

But imagination alone cannot complete the task. To understand another life, we must first have the generosity of spirit to respect its integrity and propriety, which means that we do not warp it with forced intrusions and selfish impositions. In a word, to understand Christ we must love him as a person and a friend. And he will not withhold himself from those who earnestly seek him.

Out of the silence he will speak.

☦ ☦ ☦

## 4. Two Kinds of Christian Errors

From the Bible, tradition, and Christian teachings we learn that in various ways and at sundry times it has pleased God to reveal aspects of his character. For Christians this revelation culminates in the person of God's earth-born Son. If no man has ever seen God the Father and no one can penetrate his deeper mysteries, the Christian believer has access to the mind and teachings of Christ the Son who is the very image of the Father.

Christian teachings, tradition, and biblical revelations about God mean that we have an ample foundation for a theology, or knowledge of God, which we can formulate as dogma and know intellectually. Discounting poet Heinrich Heine's caution that the moment a religion seeks the aid of philosophy its ruin is inevitable, probably Christian faith and its theology could make good use of a truly Christian philosophy. Yet even though there have been many Christians who philosophized over the ages, to my knowledge there has never been a Christian philosophy in the full sense, that is, one resting on Christian premises and not on the customary Greek principles. As philosopher Immanuel Kant remarked and Alfred North Whitehead repeated, all philosophy since the Greeks has been but footnotes to Plato and Aristotle. In reality Christianity absorbed the thought of both philosophers: Platonic, or neo-Platonic, idealism in the beginning centuries, Aristotelian logic and categories in the Middle Ages. The fact that there is no purely Christian philosophy may mean that it is simply not possible. Or perhaps it is. Perhaps it will turn out to be, as I believe, the intellectual imperative that stirs the creative Christian genius of the coming age.

The closest we have come to a "Christian" philosophy have been the Christianized versions of Aristotle's doctrines introduced and refined by Boethius, Hildegarde von Bingen, William of Ockham, St. Anselm, St. Thomas Aquinas, and the last of the great Scholastic philosophers, St. Francisco Suárez. But even though much of Aristotelian thought was compatible with Christianity and medieval scholasticism became the foundation on which the modern world rests, the Schoolmen sometimes seemed to forget that Aristotle himself was pagan, not Christian, and some, it seems, were ready to confer Christian "citizenship" on him, as they were on Seneca. Consequently, some of his doctrines introduced errors into theological thinking that persist to this day, particularly where personhood is concerned. For example, when Boethius defined the human person as *rationalis naturae individua substantia* (the rational individual substance of nature) he elevated Aristotelianism to a position of prominence in Christian theology and its subservient offshoots philosophy and science, thus beginning a tradition of understanding humankind primarily in terms of rationality.

And the assumption has endured to this day. Not only the medieval theologians but also the moderns—Descartes, Pascal, the Enlightenment physiocrats and *philosophes*, along with the nineteenth-century positivists, pragmatists, and empiricists, to mention only a few names and schools—all built their systems on the underlying assumption of human rationality. The same is true of the later existentialists and their deconstuctionist descendants, except that they flipped the rationalist coin and came up with its irrational counter face. If, as they variously argue, humankind and its acts are an irrational absurdity, that man is a joke, or victim, or byproduct of the indifferent cosmos, as the case may be, the criterion by which they reach this dubious judgment is none other than the old rationality of modern philosophy. For it stands to reason that in order to declare someone insane, absurd, or irrational, one must first know what constitutes sanity, sense, or rationality. Thanks to this unbroken and unbiblical rationalistic tradition, the scientific designation of modern mankind is *homo sapiens*, that is, "wise" or "knowing" man, in other words, man the rational creature. But can we not reason that it could have been as easily any number of alternate—and perhaps better—designations had Christian thinking developed along other lines? Neither the Bible nor the Christian tradition restricts the human person to abstract rational or irrational categories in the Aristotelian and Cartesian mode, but instead stresses the indivisible reality of the whole person.

Let us be generous and give due credit to Aristotle and the Scholastic Aristotelians. Aristotelianism was an admirable and fruitful way of thinking, but it was not wholly the Christian view of human reality that I shall attempt to sketch in broad strokes in this book.

Consider an example near our own time and place. The "Bell Curve" racial controversy of the 1990s and books like Michael Levin´s *Why Race Matters* (1997), which purport to draw out the ominous consequences of racial differences, are based on the same ancient assumption that human rationality, understood numerically as IQ in our day, is the highest and most definitive characteristic of human kind. But are there not other human qualities that could as readily, and perhaps more justifiably from a Christian perspective, define human uniqueness? I have in mind mercy, compassion, love, charity, spiritual gifts, forbearance, etc. I do not know of anything in the Gospels or in Christian tradition that defines mankind as *homo sapiens*.

The fact that Christianity is a theological religion means that it is possible to make two kinds of mistakes regarding God. We may be either religiously disobedient or fall into intellectual errors about him. Even in our irreverent age relatively few people are atheists—and most of them only when free of peril and penury. Most of us still acknowledge

God or a Supreme Being in some form, but the almost infinite fragmentation of Christianity offers more proof than we need that Christians have made countless intellectual mistakes about their faith. Of one spirit, generally speaking, we are far from being of one mind.

Theology in the Christian mold is impossible in those religions in which God wholly transcends human understanding and is, therefore, formally unknowable. Islam, for example, permits only a modest theology if taken in the sense that I define it here; Buddhism, if I understand it aright, allows none at all.

This Christian theological richness does not in and of itself argue for the veracity or superiority of the Christian faith. In some ways Greek polytheism, for instance, is more "theological" than Christianity, for we have much more information about the gods of Olympus than about the God of the Bible.

How seriously are we to take the theology of polytheistic religions and on what justifiable basis are we to reject it? Historically Christians have dismissed the matter simply by dismissing the gods themselves, thus clipping their claims at the root. Despite their best—and worst—patriotic efforts to preserve their native religion, the Romans were unable to save Jupiter and his cohort of gods from oblivion. Ultimately they could only watch in powerless alarm and outrage as the old national deities melted away like wax effigies in the rising evangelical heat of Christianity.

✝✝✝

## 5. The Absurdity of Christian Belief

Here we come to an interesting set of questions for the Christian believer: on what basis does he accept or reject the truth of Christianity itself? And what assurance is there, if any, that Christian theology is reliable, or if rejected,

unreliable? The quick answer to these questions is, for most
Protestants, faith in the Bible and the guidance of the Holy
Spirit. Others, especially Catholic or Orthodox believers,
would agree, adding Church Tradition and magisterial
teachings. But are there extra-biblical or extra-ecclesiastical
reasons that support the claims of Christianity? Here I'll
consider one method by coming at it from what may seem
an odd angle of access.

The surprising thing about much of pagan theology,
especially the Greco-Roman variety, is how easily we
understand it. Zeus, Jupiter, and their counterparts in other
pagan religions make sense to us. From our own nature we
understand their motives, lusts, hatreds, betrayals, responsibilities, and irrational acts. No wonder the Greek and
Roman gods have inspired so much art and literature.
Apart from their immortality and superhuman powers,
they are very like us and in some cases even spurn immortality to be one of us. The fact is, they are too like us, which
causes us to conclude that they are creatures of human
imagination.

On the other hand, the revelations of God often baffle us.
They do not conform to our human expectations and
motives. But he gives us fair warning: his ways are not our
ways. God never behaves like lusty Zeus or jealous Hera or
furious Ares or handsome Apollo or seductive Aphrodite.
From *Genesis* to *Revelation* his love and concern for
mankind are apparent, but his methods are a mystery, and
we cannot anticipate, as with pagan gods, what he will do
next, nor, for that matter, understand what he did last. For
this reason, even at their clearest, both the Bible narrative
and the soundest Christian theology unfold against a vast
panorama of sacred mystery too deep for human understanding.

Aristotle was aware of what I am about to write when he
declared that some stories are so improbable that this very
feature becomes evidence in their favor. And so it is with
the Christian faith. It is a story so counterintuitive, so
contrary to common sense, that this very strangeness

THE LIGHT OF EDEN

argues paradoxically for its truthfulness. For we must ask ourselves what human imagination, what human intellect could conceive of a God in three persons, equally one God and equally three persons? It defies our arithmetic, baffles our logic, and, not infrequently, outrages the skeptic. It is— dare we say it?—absurd, but so transcendentally absurd that we put aside our petty objections and bow before it in worshipful wonder. As Kierkegaard argued so well, it is not within the reasonable limits of human imagination to conceive of a plan of salvation whereby God himself comes to earth, is born of a virgin to human personhood, suffers, dies, and rises again in order to redeem mankind from eternal death. Nor can human logic accommodate the notion that the death of a crucified man signifies the defeat of death. The story of altruistic Prometheus is a bloodless fable compared to the salvation wrought by Christ. To be a Christian we must be childish enough, mature enough, and wise enough to let ourselves seem foolish. This is why, so it seems to me, the rational limits we attribute to God so as to predetermine what he can or cannot do and still be God verges on rational heresy. Such evidence as we have in these matters points to a different conclusion: rationality does not limit God; God limits rationality.

To the scandal of rationalists, the early Christian writer Tertullian (150-230 A.D.) said of Christianity that "It is believable because it is foolish" and he is also credited— perhaps wrongly—with the celebrated saying "I believe because it is absurd" (*Credo quia absurdum est*). His point is a persuasive paradox: if Christianity were more rational, it would be less believable. The Christian does not believe because Christianity is plausible but because it is humanly impossible. It is a sign of intelligence but the height of folly to try to rationalize faith. Precisely because we do not see its ways with our mind, we cannot rely on sight and insight but must walk in faith.

Christianity has always scandalized rationalists. The question for them has been what to make of the scandal. The best of them, St. Paul, for example, were drawn into it

*I / Biblical Perspectives* 23

and became scandals themselves to the rest of the pagan world. To our great good fortune, I should add. Therefore, let us pray that the Christian scandal will continue to irritate rational people so that they may come to see that what they take to be the mere foolishness of Christianity contains wisdom and glory far beyond the reach and breadth of human reason.

✝✝✝

### 6. Curious Greeks and Eccentric Christians

From biblical and extra-biblical documentation we can derive a composite picture of the first Christians. And it was not a pretty sight to non-Christians. Within the Classical world of Greece and Rome, the Judeo-Christian appeared to be incomprehensibly eccentric, so much so that a cultural abyss came to separate those lands informed by the Judeo-Christian spirit from those that were not. And the differences continue even to this day. As Catholic philosopher Julián Marías observes in *The Christian Perspective*, merely by being, or having been Christian or Jew the believer bears within himself a unique view of reality. Quite independent of Christian faith itself, which may indeed be residual or even extinguished, one becomes aware of certain aspects of reality and organizes them into hierarchies that are characteristic of the Christian perspective. Likewise one is sensitized to certain forms of moral evidence and obligation and accepts the validity of proofs that otherwise would pass unnoticed.

This sensitivity, therefore, is not primarily a matter of intelligence but of perspective. The Greeks, to whom we are eternally indebted, may have been the most intelligent people who ever lived, and in so many ways and so readily we imitate their philosophical reasoning, enlightened curiosity, and probing skepticism. What Heraclitus or Plato or Aristotle said we ourselves could have argued only yesterday and indeed may have done so in one version or another. Yet as Christianized or once-Christianized persons we are repulsed to learn that apparently without a second thought people of this enlightened race abandoned their unwanted infants to be eaten by wild beasts.

The Greeks did not teach well—perhaps because they were too intelligent to understand well—that intellect must be the servant of ethics, not its master. For this lesson we must turn to the Judeo-Christian dimension of our cultural heritage, which did not, and does not, cease to teach us this priority. Compassion, brotherhood, forbearance, humility, forgiveness, charity, and love are not unknown qualities in other faiths and cultures, but in the Judeo-Christian tradition they rise to the dignity of primary moral imperatives. The Greek could abandon his unwanted child without prejudice to his ethical self-esteem. The Jew and the Christian cannot. To let a beggar die in the street may be a matter of indifference to those religions whose ultimate aim is to free us from being altogether. But for the Judeo-Christian to do so would be a violation of the moral and religious imperative to cherish human life. The Judeo-Christian can be wicked, and often is, but knowing the law of love towards his fellow men, he is convicted by the awareness of his wickedness. He may slay his brother or his neighbor but he cannot walk away from the deed with the Greek's primitive peace of mind. He knows better, and his evil is infinitely greater because he knows.

✝✝✝

### 7. The Judeo-Christian Tradition and Other Considerations

Probably we speak too glibly these days of the so-called "Judeo-Christian" tradition. (The hyphen itself serves as a shorthand symbol of the disjunctive link between the Jew and the Christian; it reminds us of both their ineradicable bond and definitive break.) Obviously there is continuity between Judaism and Christianity; Christians believe that the Old Testament foreshadows Christianity and the New Testament fulfills the Old and, further, that neither can be fully understood apart from the other. They testify to each other. But the link between Judaism and Christianity was not originally theological. The first Jewish theological writings appeared after the initial Christian theology of apostles John and Paul.

This tardiness is understandable if we keep in mind that the original Jewish understanding of God was not theological but covenantal. God was real to the Hebrews and their Jewish descendants because he was faithful to his Covenant with the Chosen People. On the other hand, Christianity was always a deeply theological religion because of the ample and intimate revelations about God by his Son.

The worldviews of the two related faiths were almost reverse images of each other when they parted ways near the end of the first century A.D. In order to survive, Judaism withdrew in introverted isolation from surrounding pagan cultures, and even though it officially welcomed proselytes—even to the point of sending out missionaries—it did so with misgivings, as we see in the book of *Jonah*. And no wonder; we know from the Bible that with few exceptions its contacts with other cultures were unfortunate. On the other hand, the very survival of Christianity depended upon its evangelization of Gentiles. Its brightest moments have ever been times of expansion. As the culminating act of his earthly sojourn, Christ himself launched his disciples on the so-called "Great Commission," which was nothing less than the conversion of the *oikoumene*, or entire inhabited earth. Unlike the Jew who jealously defended the truth of God against the power of paganism, the Christian zealously undertook to overcome paganism by the power of God's truth to call people out of the darkness. The Jew spurned the world because he was

Jewish; the Christian converted it because he was Christian. But does any of this matter today? In these so-called post-modern and post-Christian times can one be intellectually responsible and believe in God or accept the Bible as his word? But the better question would be, is it possible to live in unbelief? At first the answer seems obvious: millions of people have given up their Christian beliefs. Or so it seems, but perhaps not, if we look more closely. It is a general paradox of our age that many things are taken for granted that are simply impossible. The denial of Christianity and the embrace of skepticism is itself a deficient form of belief. Both make sense of a sort only when we presuppose a prior faith.

Finally, I know of no good reason not to enjoy this exploration of the Christian world view. It is incomprehensible to me how one can write willingly of matters that do not correspond to some deep well of joy. As a matter of the world's accustomed course we may be certain that grim problems will always beset us and that calamity holds a strong claim to our lives. Sensitive to this plight, some think it wrong to be happy as long as humanity suffers. But this attitude would condemn us all to endless gloom, and as Christians we must ask whether it is right for us to add our willful misery to the world's sad state. For, after all, we are the children of promise, and this everlasting assurance gives us joy greater than our problems and happiness beyond our understanding. A sympathetic philosopher might describe the experience as an ontological shift to a new state of being, and he would be right; and the skeptic would call it an affront to common sense, and he, too, would be right. But both miss the central vision: in the darkness of the world and in the very pain of life we have seen a great light of deliverance, a divine light, what I have called *The Light of Eden*.

And the darkness cannot overcome it.

# II

## TRUTH AND ITS RELATIVES

Skeptical Pontius Pilate asked Jesus, "What is truth?" So saying and hearing no response from his prisoner, he walked away from Truth and into everlasting infamy.

☩ ☩ ☩

## 8. Pilate's Error

Pilate's question was already a cliché in his day, one the Greek philosophers had been asking and debating for hundreds of years. The Greek thinkers presupposed that within or behind or beyond the surface appearance and accidental features of things abided their "true" unchanging nature. Called by many names over the ages—*physis, ousia, entelécheia, substantia,* essence, being, idea, the thing-in-itself, etc.—this elusive proto-reality and the efforts to discover it have dominated philosophical thinking for more than twenty-five centuries.

In much the same spirit today science continues the hunt for the tiniest particles of matter. So elusive are these ultimate subdivisions of matter that theoretical physics now seems to be lodged in a no man's land between materiality and metaphysics.

To the Greeks truth corresponded to an abstract *what?* Truth came from reducing complex things to governing principles, definitions, and constituent parts. From these Greek thinkers we inherited the procedures of rational analysis, dissection, and the assumption that the more a thing is reduced to its components, the closer we come to its essence and thus the "truer" it becomes, for they thought the indivisible part was purer than the complex amalgam. It was a magnificent intellectual legacy and when coupled with its antipodal sister concept of synthesis, made possible the splendor of Western science and philosophy. But our inheritance has also been a tether; like a golden chain around the ankle of Western mankind, its slack lets us go only so far before it jerks taut and leaves us no choice but to pace back and forth at its full extent. The history of Western thought is an ancient pathway trodden deep by many generations of thinkers, captive to the foundational Greek assumptions.

For the Christian believer Pilate asked the wrong question and in one of the supreme ironies of history, squandered the rare privilege of perceiving the answer physically and personally present before him. For the Christian question is not *What*, but *Who* is truth? And the Christian answer is Christ, for *truth is a person*, truth incarnate, truth made flesh, living truth. We Christians said these words in the beginning; we have said them ever since. Whether we have ever understood our words remains an open question.

Like almost all known early cultures, the pre-Classical Greeks resorted to divination in order to regulate their activities and determine the best times for future undertakings. By examining the entrails of sacrificial victims or heeding the oracles at Delphi and Dodona they believed they could anticipate future events and make their plans accordingly.

But often the omens were slow to reveal themselves and the oracles frequently so garbled as to frustrate the best laid plans of men. In his military campaign in Calpe, in Asiatic Thrace, for example, Xenophon's army all but starved, and many of his soldiers were slaughtered by the enemy as sacrifice after sacrifice failed to yield the favorable omen to advance. There was a perilous discontinuity between the urgencies of the campaign and the imponderable mysteries of the hidden realm that shaped the deeds of men.

Perplexed by these unpredictable signs and the ever-changing shape of things, eventually the Greeks began to search for more reliable predictors than sacrificial entrails and delirious sibyls. Amidst all the mutations and uncertainties of the world they needed to know the unchanging, reliable nature of things so as to anticipate their behavior and attune their own accordingly.

This practical need to know the essence of things gave rise to the early speculations of Greek philosophy and science. Philosophy was born of human perplexity, and to this day the problems of authentic philosophy are those of perplexed people. The rest is sophistry. Understood from this perspective, truth in the first instance is the fidelity of things to their nature or principle, what was called *arché* and which manifests itself in a revelatory, illuminating moment of truth (*alétheia*).

✝✝✝

9. The Case of the Drowning Swimmer

On the other hand, the Christian began from an existential perspective of life that was even more drastic and radical than the Greek dilemma. If the Greek philosophized because of a collective need to know the predictable nature and behavior of things, the Christian looked on the world with a sense of personal inadequacy and lostness. After all, most of the earliest Christian converts were slaves, women, disempowered Jews, and other persecuted groups who had little control of their earthly destiny. Whereas the Greek desired intellectual certainty about the world, the Christian sought personal salvation from its burdens and snares. The Greek marveled at the world and wanted to know it; the Christian distrusted it because he knew it only too well.

Consequently, the Greek exhibited an intellectual self-sufficiency that is entirely lacking in the conquered Jew and

subjugated Christian. The Greek, like the modern rationalists, confidently believed that with mind alone he could
encompass and unravel the enigmas of reality, unlike the
Christian and Jew who assumed that certain mysteries transcended human intellect and corresponded only to faith in
God. The Greek exaltation of personal sufficiency manifested itself in several ways, from the apotheosis of the
human form in art and athletic contests to the unparalleled
prowess of the Greek intellect in its far-ranging philosophical speculations. The exuberance of Greek thought was
contagious and the aesthetic splendor of Greek art almost
irresistible. Both Jew and Christian felt its seductive attraction and to some extent fell under its sway. The world had
never seen anything like Greek creativity at its peak and
after its passing, would not see its likes again for nearly two
thousand years in the age dubiously called the High
Renaissance.

Despite certain ethical traits in common with the Classical
Greeks and Romans, especially the later Stoics, the Christian
believer was a transformed person, in the words of Christ
himself, one born again. Much less curious than the Greek
about the nature and behavior of material things, though
concerned for them as their caretaker, the believer looked
beyond this present time to the apocalyptic consummation
of time itself. After all, though terribly concrete and
problem-haunted, the world was finally unsubstantial, a
temporary stage on which the divine drama was being
acted out only so long as it pleased God. To the Christian, as
to his Jewish religious forebears, only the Divine was truly
real and truly trustworthy.

From the Christian perspective, as the branch cut from
the vine withers, so mankind separated from the Creator
perishes. Therefore, man's primary urgency is not so much
to understand the nature of materiality as it is to seek a
saving relationship with Christ. Alone, he is like a shipwrecked sailor who finds himself perilously adrift in the
ocean. Unlike the high-spirited Greek, he struggles in dread
of imminent doom. The modern existential philosophers

from Kierkegaard to Heidegger spoke, and correctly so, of the anguish of lost man.

Here we find another of the several ironies of the Christian condition. Unlike the Greek who puts his trust in intellect, the Christian acknowledges his immoral and mental shortcomings and counts himself unworthy in his fallen state. But once renewed in faith and sustained by the *Paraclete*, the Holy Spirit, he makes an even greater boast than the Greek: he declares with St. Paul that nothing can separate him from the divine love and that he can do all things through Christ who strengthens him.

Whatever the Christian initially loses in intellectual self-sufficiency he gains in drama. Not that this drama consists of the external risks of the soldier or contrived dangers of the adventurer or the athlete. Rather it is the innate but cosmic tragedy of the fallen human condition, what philosopher Miguel de Unamuno called in his great book by the same title "the tragic sense of life." Afloat in the existential ocean amidst the general human calamity, the shipwrecked sailor has no choice but to strike out in desperation for the distant shore. He either makes the effort or he perishes. He must sink or swim.

As he swims for shore the struggling sailor finds about him debris from the shipwreck. Some of it is solid and trustworthy and may help to keep him afloat for a time, but other things that at first appear dependable are unreliable, that is, untrue, and will not bear his weight.

Despite his best efforts, the shore is too far and the sailor's human strength is soon spent. The wreckage of the shipwreck, his local and limited truth, keeps him afloat only so long. As predators close in to devour him and he sinks exhausted into the depths he cries out for help, and a spike-scarred divine hand reaches down and lovingly offers to lift him from the water. He reaches up in acceptance and is saved.

Here we see the primary Christian meaning of truth. Truth is the Divine Person, the Savior, who comes to us in our lost condition and saves us from certain death. At this personal level Truth is always redemptive, always a saving truth. And redemptive truth vibrates in our heart with its own convincing power that falsehood for all its disguises can only imitate but never match. But there is a further dimension to the drama of personal salvation. God does not merely rescue us from peril and deposit us on a safe shore there to resume our old life. Whomever he saves he exalts and whatever he touches bears his imprint forever. To be saved is to experience a renaissance of life, a rebirth, and to be reborn is to be born to a higher life. The Christian resigns himself to releasing the good so that he can gain the best.

This means that unlike the capricious gods of the pagans or even the remote deistic God of the modern rationalists, the God of Christianity for all his unspeakable majesty and unapproachable light is never far from us. Despite his humbleness of station in this world, the Christian lives in the shadow of the sacred, and this divine proximity and continuous fatherly concern for the believer confer on human life a hallowed, invulnerable dignity. Though worldly powers and potentates may belittle him and hold him as naught, he knows that he matters and matters infinitely, to no less than the very Creator. He can treasure his soul for it has been redeemed with a king's ransom and rescued by a loving truth beyond telling.

There are other levels of truth, or at least what we with our imprecise languages call truth. There are useful truths like the serviceable flotsam from the shipwreck. Beyond them lies a vast category of truth that we describe commonly as facts, data, or details. For example, it is "true," as we would commonly say, that the desperate sailor finds himself immersed in a liquid called water, which has a molecular composition of two hydrogen atoms to one of oxygen and which covers the earth to an unknown depth as far as he can see. And it is true that Betelgeuse, a star of the first magnitude and the largest in the Constellation Orion, shines down on him from a distance of several light years. But far from being saving, redemptive truths, these are impersonal data that are beside the fact of his immediate peril.

THE LIGHT OF EDEN

We can speculate that when the world fell, truth and fact became tragically separated. Fact was enmeshed in materiality, while truth withdrew into ideality. The imperative is, and always has been, the restoration of their unity. For in this way, as we suspect, begins the salvation of the world and the plenary restoration of human life. The world needs me in my restored integrity in order to be fully a world, and I need the re-harmonized world in order to be fully myself. I shall take up this theme in a stronger way near the end of this book.

In the redemptive sense that we have just seen, truth leads us to more truth and unless abandoned, always to the divine truth. From it we depart and to it we return at the end of things. Even though because of our ignorance there may be perceived gaps in its universal integrity, there are, truthfully speaking, no isolated truths. Instead, every truth has an affinity—we could say a love, we could say an erotic yearning—for other truths. They come to one another's aid, linking, sustaining, rescuing, and healing persons, communities, nations, systems, worlds. Truth bonds, sin separates, and fact can be the indifferent servant of both. This is why in the long run it is impossible to live in error yet serve truth. In order to be true, life and labor must be of a piece.

From the beginning of the Modern Age it has been a working hypothesis that we can discover truth by testing and discarding error. Truth, we suppose with good common sense, must be what remains after we have tried and proved false all other alternatives. But higher truth, personal, redemptive truth, seldom walks in step with common sense and its methods, and theologies that seek it in this way seldom go very far. Superbly useful technical data may emerge from this experimental methodology, as modern science has shown, but it is secondary, capable only of dealing with the material world and only indirectly and distantly touching the higher realities of personhood and redemption.

In our day many believe *in* the Divine Truth but few believe him. To believe God is to entrust our life to him in living faith and consuming obedience; it is to live and move and have our being in him, as St. Paul writes. On the other hand, to believe *in* God usually means, despite the misleading preposition, to acknowledge the divine reality with an inert faith and from a certain reserved distance. From afar we bow to God but live as we please—without pleasing him as we live. This is not a moral or religious accusation of modern shortcomings. For it was ever thus. Here it serves not as a condemnation of the times but as a marker on our way to other considerations.

† † †

## 10. Ideas and Beliefs in Perspective

The point we need to consider here is that a conscious belief *in* God is not wholly a belief but at least partially an idea. And all ideas are problematic, that is, prone to problems. For regardless of how exalted, ingenious, or passionate they are, ideas are mental creations whose being consists principally in being thought. They are things of an ideal sort but not the thing thought, and the distance between things and the things we say about them may be tragically or comically huge, as the history of philosophy shows.

Naturally, as sincere persons we do not quite believe what I have just written. Unless we are hypocrites, cowards, or liars, we offer our ideas not as ideas but as truth, that is, as accurate and honest facsimiles of reality itself. A third quality is even more defining: despite our civilized and civil deference to the ideas of others, we think in our heart that only ours are the true portrayals of reality.

But anything humanly said risks being humanly wrong. Our ideas may falsify reality because they arise from a false perspective such as a perverse ideology or demonic religion and not from our own authentic view of reality. Even more commonly, they may contain a valid truth but one stretched beyond its applicable limits. And the more an idea intrudes invalidly into regions of life where it has no business the more obsessive it becomes. Who has not known people so maniacally consumed by a single idea that it warps their entire understanding of the world?

We see the world with our ideas and think them to be true, but once framed in consciousness—ours or anyone's—they are subject to comparisons, modifications, and displacements. Sooner or later, a better idea—or perhaps for the maniac, a more maniacal one—may happen along to seduce people into replacing an older notion. Ideas are flimsy in their loyalty and duration, which must surely be why we come by them so easily and replace them so readily.

Unlike ideas, beliefs, like the subsoil, are normally invisible and unknown. We do not hold them as we hold ideas or opinions. Instead they hold us, for we live within them normally as unaware of their presence as fish are of water or as we are of the gravity that holds our feet to the ground. "As he thinketh in his heart, so is he..." (*Proverbs*: 23:7). We are what we believe.

One of the great fables of the Modern Age was the idea of objectivity, the notion that we can remove obstructions between our senses and reality and perceive things as they really are. Nothing could be less likely. As Heraclitus said ages ago, nature is secretive. It does not appear in nude frankness but comes before us in modesty, already primped by ideas and dressed in beliefs. We could say that reality always strikes a believable pose before us. I said we see the world with our ideas; now I must add that *the world we see with our ideas is reality conformed to the architectural structure of our beliefs.*

Beliefs give us a primary domestication of things, a working metaphysics that allows us to make initial sense of them. Without beliefs reality would appear to us, as it must appear to a baby, as a bewildering, even terrifying, chaos of light, sound, and movement. We see what we believe, and we cannot interpret what our sight tells us if our beliefs cannot accommodate what we see. Ask anyone who has been lost in a wilderness.

Confronted with an utterly new and alien reality, either we translate it into a known category of things and deny its differences or we treat it as a violation of the rules of reality and tradition, as a fabulous or demonic aberration, as the American Indians did when they saw the first European horsemen, or as the skeptical Pharisees and Sadducees who witnessed the miracles of Jesus but could not accommodate them to their beliefs. Perhaps children do not remember their first encounters with reality because they have not yet internalized the beliefs necessary for channeling and interpreting things. Beliefs enable us to classify things and to that extent, to exert a certain hierarchical control over them. On the other hand, like the imperceptible "dark matter" of the universe, non-believed things glide by like unseen phantoms before our senses, for we are blind to what our beliefs do not contain. Objectivity, therefore, is not a feature of the world but a dimension of a certain form of belief.

For these reasons, real beliefs, those that are unconscious assumptions of reality itself, have very little to do with the popular concept of competing "belief systems," which for the most part are not beliefs at all but consciously held ideas, or in a more complex form, ideologies. But it would be a mistake to say that there is no connection at all. Since the eighteenth-century Enlightenment, and to a lesser degree since the Protestant Reformation two hundred years earlier, the West has lived on a steady diet of ideas and their practical manifestations we call technologies. Periodically, they march aggressively out of the West in imperialistic conquest of the world. Paradoxically, we could say that it was an unquestioned belief in ideas that helped shape the Modern West and, by aggressive penetration, the rest of the world.

This long phase of Western history may be ending. In our day the prestige of ideas has begun to slip. Not that their numbers have decreased. On the contrary, we are awash in ideas, ours and others, but we believe in them less and

consider them to be disposable. Like currency in infla-
tionary cycles, they have diminished value. The world again
grows weary of rational thinking. Oswald Spengler's old
prediction that the West is about to revert to a cult of blood
may be coming to pass.

While beliefs are by definition unconscious at the deepest
level, ideas have an evident intellectual pedigree and
profile. They must be consciously learned and taught. This
requires writers, teachers, books, and schools. As one would
expect, therefore, the rise of ideas in the Modern Age coin-
cided with the growth of publishing and modern universities. For even though both had existed in the Middle Ages
access to them was limited and their first function was to
transmit traditional, belief-based knowledge and dogma.
The notion of fabricating new ideas was looked on as need-
less frivolity or even possible heresy. Established authority,
not the pursuit of new knowledge, was the foundation of
medieval learning.

† ✝ †

## 11.  Dogma and Belief

Religious beliefs and dogmas, especially those of
Christian extraction, have long suffered from a bad press.
Yet beliefs are usually more forgiving and humane than the
ideas or facts, or pseudo-facts, summoned to defend or
demolish them. The slander usually attributed to Voltaire
that more people have died in the name of Christianity than
in all the wars of history is an example of an anti-dogmatic
falsehood endlessly repeated. Usually what we think of as
beliefs and dogma are the imperious ideas that attach to
them and not infrequently usurp them, as cancerous cells
invade normal tissue. As a consequence of its unsavory
reputation there are calls to alter and abandon Christian
dogma in the name of freedom. To do so, as many have

done, is a cruel and misguided irony, for dogma is the earthly repository and font of true freedom, the freedom to be who we ought to be. For where, one must ask, has sustained freedom existed outside the Judeo-Christian tradition? Nowhere I know of. Yet there will be calls to liberalize Christian dogma until people realize that dogma is the only liberalizing power in the world today.

We are dealing with sensitive difficulties. Let us proceed with what appears to be a play on words: many forms of Christian toleration have become intolerable to believers and harmful to non-believers. In the first instance Christianity does not offer toleration of sin or wrongdoing but qualities of incomparable superiority: forgiveness, charity, love of one's enemies, and the good news of redemption. It is a tepid Christianity that forgets itself and embraces wrong without reminder of right, and a weak faith indeed that extends fellowship to evil without urging repentance.

Tolerance makes its appearance when Christian belief has weakened to the inferior level of ideas. True Christian beliefs have everything to do with benevolence and very little with modern tolerance because, as we have seen, they are the face of reality itself. It is true that Christian beliefs have a conscious dimension to them as well, summed up and repeated in creeds, prayers, liturgy, and scriptural teachings. But normally they are but the verbal surface of unconscious beliefs that underlie and inform all dimensions of life. This is what we have been calling the Christian perspective.

If we analyze our beliefs, and we can only do so comparatively, we discover that in most cases they reveal varying degrees of contradiction and disorder. What we believe in one area of life may be opposed to what we believe in another. Sometimes the conflicts are so great as to reduce us to psychological paralysis. This is particularly true in recent times with its mixed messages and clashing ideologies. On the one hand, for example, we believe in Christian charity, but on the other, we have internalized the competitive message to beat "the other guy" and see that "Number One" comes out on top even if winning means committing unethical acts.

Nevertheless, as we probe deeper we will discover eventually a master belief that informs all the others and places them in a vital hierarchy. In many cases this discovery does not come easily and it may take a life crisis to bring into focus what we really believe—perhaps to our own surprise and to the astonishment of those about us. Psychologically speaking, Christian conversion truly occurs when our acceptance of Christ becomes our master belief on which all other beliefs depend subordinately and, alternatively, from which false beliefs are purged.

✝✝✝

## 12. Media, Ideas, and Green Fruit

Although it was not always so, in our time we associate the media with the "news," which for the most part consists of a daily recitation of the world's horrors. Shall we forget that the world got along for thousands of years without anything resembling the media—and probably could do so again? We accuse them, right and left, of bias and a lack of objectivity. But by their very nature, or at least the nature imposed on them, *the media cannot be objective.*

Because of the nature of our beliefs, human perceptions are not objective to begin with. But that concept is too abstract to be of much help in this discussion, so we need to examine the media from another perspective.

The fact that the media report the "news," means that normal things remain unreported. For "news" to be new, a context of normalcy is necessary. If all people were murderers, murder would not be news, and if lying and thievery were the norm, then truth and honesty would be newsworthy scandals. Normalcy makes the news possible by remaining invisible. Only by presupposing the general good behavior of people and the orderly march of things do the world's crimes, calamities, and violence become newsworthy. "If it bleeds, it reads," the crass journalistic saying goes, but this is because most things do not bleed. Customarily, the media do not report normal happenings—which is almost everything—but what is abnormal, that is, "new."

The problem with the news is that subject to a daily diet of the abnormal, we lose sight of the normal order of circumstances and mistake the inverted and the perverted for the real. When this happens, we begin to live reality as fiction and assume that our world is sliding headlong into irreparable degeneracy. In the end we may succumb to the dark certainty that we live in the worst of times with the worst of people and that any past time was better. Even random natural calamities may come to be seen as part of a general conspiracy of disorder against humanity.

The antidote for the fictional reality of the media is a healthy dose of reality itself. If we ignore the media and their horrific anomalies and consider instead our experiences with neighbors, friends, and fellow workers, we discover that many of them—probably a majority—are reasonably decent and courteous, in short, much like people have always been and disarmingly like us in their vices and virtues.

Probably, the media have inflicted their greatest harm on the ideas of our time. Time was when ideas spread slowly. People had to await the occasional arrival of couriers, criers, travelers, prophets, or other informed persons to discover what was happening and what people were thinking abroad. As late as the French Revolution, we read that days passed before people living in the outlying districts of Paris learned about the epochal events that had occurred in their city. The unhurried pace of life meant that for most of human history ideas germinated slowly; long periods of time passed as they were discussed, debated, sifted, modified, polished, refined, and digested. No one has argued better than Anglican-turned-Catholic Henry Cardinal Newman the wisdom of giving ideas—especially good ideas—a long time to gestate and grow to useful maturity. In marked contrast, today no sooner does an idea appear on the horizon than it is rushed like unripened fruit to the public market. Three consequences, all regrettable, happen as a result: first, instead of working their way though the censoring, polishing social process of debate and discussion, most ideas are fixed in the public consciousness in an immature state; second, many ideas are rejected not because they are inherently bad but because they are thrust on the public stage before their time has come; and third, once planted in the public mind, these unpolished ideas frequently pass into ordinance and law while simultaneously deepening into the unquestioned assumptions we call beliefs. Probably much of the crudeness of contemporary legislation, thought, and behavior begins by force feeding the public poorly reasoned, poorly digested ideas.

✝✝✝

## 13. Summary Comparisons

Christian conversion is a conscious experience, but it reaches far below consciousness to restructure one's entire understanding of life. We see the world in a new light. But the remaking of our life takes time. Not even the most dramatic conversion, such as St. Paul's, consists of a single experience but instead involves a dynamic and complementary series of further deepening conversions, what many Christians call spiritual growth. Following his conversion, Saul continued to be Saul the Jew, but it was as Paul the Roman and apostle to the Gentiles that history was to remember him. This shift of emphasis reminds us that as Abram became Abraham and the fictional Alonso Quijana or Quesada was transformed into Don Quixote, their condition was radically and forever altered. Paul reports that he spent at least three years, perhaps longer, in study and contemplation before he began his active ministry. As Christians, we die daily to ourselves and every day we are reborn in greater conformity to Christ. This transformation is beyond our natural power. Compared to the *natural* beliefs we saw earlier that allow us to deal primarily with material reality, Christian beliefs could be described as *supernatural,* and they allow us to begin living an exalted life even while we are still in the natural world. As Christians we live already in eternity.

But what does it mean concretely to speak of accepting Christ? The inquiring Jewish lawyer in the Gospel of Matthew repeats the answer: "Thou shalt love the Lord thy God with all thy heart, and with all thy soul, and with all thy strength, and with all thy mind; and thy neighbor as thyself" (*Matthew* 10:27). The Jewish believer shared the Christ-given commandment to love God and neighbor, but he could not accept the trans-Jewish concept of neighbor that Jesus had begun to teach. The Jew looked on Samaritans, Romans, Greeks, and Gentiles of every tribe and nation not as neighbors but as outsiders and real or potential adversaries.

For the Christian, Christ personally embodies or incarnates the Way, the Truth, and the Life in God (*John* 14:6). Literally he fleshes out the double imperative regarding God and neighbor and by doing so supersedes the commonsense Jewish doctrine of that time which consisted of loving God and despising one's enemies (*Matthew* 5:43-44). It is still the way of common sense, but it was never the way of Christ.

Nor did it have to be the way of Islam, Christianity's alter ego and bitterest enemy for that reason. In fairness to the younger religion we must acknowledge that Islam claimed to be, and perhaps could have been, a further, faithful refinement of Judaism and Christianity. If we take the word in its etymological Arabic root, Christians and Jews are also "Moslems," that is, those who live in submission to God, and all are "people of the Book." They do not believe the same things, but they believe in the same way. They disagree and all the more because all three religions share the basis of their disagreement. Hence the special relationships—and the intense forms of antagonisms—that both bind and divide them.

But here these paradoxical similarities stop and the profound differences separating these kindred religions begin. Judaism could survive only through its ethnic and covenantal isolation. We read in *Isaiah* 9:2 that "The people that walked in darkness have seen a great light." But even though the Hebrews were the people chosen to receive that light and reveal it to a benighted world, throughout their history they shared it grudgingly lest it be dimmed by Gentile paganism. Jonah's fish-bellied reluctance to convey God's warning to Nineveh and his loathing of its people were common, if not correct, Jewish attitudes. On the other hand, as I said earlier, the very existence of Christianity depended on its missionary zeal. It had to transcend Judaism in order not to be reabsorbed by it. Judaism always looked inward just as Christianity very early looked outward "to the uttermost parts of the earth"—including by name even the despised Samaritans in its vision. Christianity sprouted from the seedbed of Judaism, itself a component of what historian Arnold Toynbee called the complex "compost" of near Eastern "magi" culture, but it was new religious flora conditioned but neither confined nor defined by antecedent cultures and religions.

As for Islam, originally viewed by both Judaism and Christianity as a heresy against them, it looked outward not only with the missionary expansionism of the Christian but also with an imperialistic zeal peculiar to the Moslem. Unlike Christianity, which for centuries spread surreptitiously among the humbler classes, the Moslems quickly stormed over the Near East and Northern Africa as military conquerors. Unlike the politically powerless Christians who for centuries suffered martyrdom for their faith, the triumphant Moslem armies liberally inflicted it instead in the name of Allah, and though in some cases a minority they were never a despised sect like the early Christians. Christianity yet bears the imprint of its early cultural humility, just as despite its later humiliations Islam still retains its original conquering pride and sense of victorious destiny. Furthermore, the rapid spread of Islam did not substantially alter its fundamentalist insularity. The Wahhabi, Koreish, and related tribes from the Arabian Peninsula formed the Arabic aristocracy of the vast Islamic world. Arabic remained its sacred language, and many orthodox Moslems still deem it a sacrilege to translate the Koran into other tongues. Indeed, it is said that its linguistic perfection simply cannot be rendered in other tongues. Despite its wide geographical expansion, the Islamic center has remained fixed in its original homeland.

On the other hand, both Judaism and Christianity were displaced from their birthplace and obliged to migrate both geographically and linguistically across several cultural divides. Yet what they lost in homogeneity they gained in richness and adaptability. This was particularly true of Christianity, which unlike Judaism was not anchored and fixed in a long history. Because it could not remain where it was, it could not continue to be what it was: a first-century Ebionite sect or similar offshoot of Judaism.

At first a similar enrichment occurred within Islam. Fueled by the remnants of Greek, Hebrew, Mesopotamian, Roman, and Egyptian civilizations, Islam in its youth made spectacular advances in astronomy, medicine, science, philosophy, and architecture. But these splendors eventually stagnated as its external stimulants were exhausted and recurrent waves of desert fundamentalism chilled its creative genius.

Looking at Islam from the Christian perspective, we ponder whether the privilege of retaining its hereditary ties to Arabia was a boon or a burden. Christians have a nostalgic reverence for first-century Palestine but are not bound to it. On the other hand, by turning towards Mecca in both prayer and pilgrimage does not the devout Moslem renew his obeisance to seventh-century Arabia? Chronologically the youngest of the Near Eastern religions, today Islam is the oldest in spirit. Anyone who reads contemporary Islamic writings can hardly fail to be struck by a tone reminiscent of the earliest Christian texts. Whereas Christ appears today wreathed in rich accretions of history, theology, art, and culture, it is as if Mohammed had lived only yesterday and that nothing—or surprisingly little—had happened in the fourteen intervening centuries. And in a certain sense, this sensation points to a truth: much time has passed and much has transpired but nothing substantial has happened to Islam. It is hard to escape the impression that by remaining where it was Islam has continued to be what it was. Contemporary fundamentalist branches of Christianity make the same claim but lack the confirming historical continuity.

Does this mean, finally, that Christianity must choose between cultural toleration and religious intolerance? Should it copy the way of the world and withdraw its gospel or go in the opposite direction and adopt the aggressive tactics of its younger rival Islam in spreading its message? The questions are misleading, which is why they are perennial temptations for Christians to resist. True Christianity, that is, Christianity that is true to Christ, is neither tolerant nor intolerant. And for this reason Christians know in their better moments that the transcendent way of the Cross cannot be the sensible way of the Crescent. By sensible conquest that every conqueror understands and repeats, Islam acquired a vast worldly *imperium* to its credit. But the way of the Cross is a calling to a higher kingdom not primarily of this world yet destined to take root and grow in the world. The Christianized countries have often succumbed to the same imperial temptations as Moslems, yet Christians cannot escape the sobering reminder that even if they gain the whole world they are at risk of losing their souls in the conquest.

As we Christians see it, our faith offers the best hope in this world and the next. As for non-Christians, it serves neither their interests nor ours for us to hide our Christianity under a basket lest its light offend them. Nor does it do them or us any good at all to compromise with the passing mischief of this world. On the contrary, by remaining true to Christ, as Christ is true to us, Christians create the humane conditions that allow non-Christians to dwell in peace, prosperity, and dignity in our midst. In their hearts non-Christians know this to be true. If it were not so they would not come amongst us to live in the first place. They do not often say so in open gratitude with their lips, for loyalty to their own creeds forbids it, but they offer stronger testimony with their feet.

Neither lapsed Christians nor non-Christians could long tolerate the de-Christianized world they desire, for the alternatives to the Light of the World, the Light of Eden, are what history has always shown them to be: darkness, evil, and tyranny.

# III

## VARIETIES OF ANTHROPOLOGY

Let me confine the term to our context. By *anthropology* I do not mean the current scientific version, which focuses preferentially on the world's few remaining stone-age cultures. Instead, I use the word in its original meaning of a general theory, or science of mankind. It includes equally the suburbanite in the mall and the savage in the muck.

✝✝✝

### 14. Mankind in Nature: Two Hypotheses

The vestigial human groups that obsess anthropologists are sometimes called "Children of the Dawn," but probably it would be more accurate to call them "Children of the Dusk," for their numbers dwindle towards extinction due to encroachments by modern men. Scientists who study them assume that for uncounted millennia these stone-age primitives have lived as they do today and that in them we see repeated and perpetuated the life of our remotest ancestors. This fascination is as understandable as the assumption itself is questionable. However, there are two alternate and compelling hypotheses.

First, the fact—if it is a fact—that these groups are still primitive after all these millennia should tell us that something about them is amiss and that they are not normal primitives and therefore their culture is not normative of prehistoric cultures. They are not the missing link, but they do appear to have a link missing. Their arrested development sheds little light on the etiology of advanced cultures, on the reasons why one fine eon ago mankind renounced its age-old companionship with the rain, mud, flies, parasites, snakes, predators, and assorted terrors, walked out of the jungle, and began to build villages and towns. Freud wrote that the purpose of civilization is to protect us from nature. The lack of cultural development among contemporary primitives suggests that they are no more indicative of normal humanity than a midget is of normal adulthood.

Second, can we be sure that today's primitives have always been primitive? Could we not suppose as plausibly that from a more advanced state they reverted to savagery? Writer Robert D. Kaplan speaks of "reprimitivized" men lately appearing in countries with "failed jurisdictions." Even in the relatively few centuries of recorded history there are many examples of cultural regression and enough evidence to suggest that decline may be the rule and progress the happy exception in human societies. Not many generations after the age of Pericles, simpleminded Greek farmers were plowing near the magnificent Athenian structures wherein their enlightened ancestors had sculpted, built, and philosophized. Seeing the gigantic aqueducts, bridges, theaters, and fortifications left by the Roman engineers, some medieval peoples concluded that the Romans must have been giants, for no mere people like themselves would be capable of such prodigies. In an early Spanish document it is reported that upon hearing the gospel from the Spanish priests, Aztec ruler Moctezuma admitted that in a former age his people heard those higher truths and lifted their hearts to God. Later, interpreting the words with gross literalism, the priests cut out their victims' hearts and held them aloft to the gods. Ethnologists describe a tribe in the Amazon rain forest that having forgotten how to make fire designates a person to guard the precious embers. Mysterious structures scattered over the earth—witness the Maya or the Zimbabweans—are testimony to advanced peoples whose descendants preserve no memory of how their forefathers achieved such splendors.

Nature always waits in ambush, eager to re-enslave humanity and condemn it anew to close companionship with the rain, mud, flies, parasites, snakes, predators, and assorted terrors. Nothing human is ever completely safe from the lurking jungle. If mankind is capable of advancement and progress it is also susceptible to relapse and decline. We play with nature at our peril.

† † †

## 15. The View from Paradise

The most exalted anthropology we know of begins in *Genesis*. Unlike many pagan accounts of creation in which good and evil contended for supremacy, good alone was active in the biblical version. Following ascending levels of creation God completed his masterpiece in an act of effusive, surpassing love. "Male and female created he them." As the culmination of the creation cycle, which God pronounced "very good" (*hineh tov me'od*), mankind was vastly superior to other living forms. Unlike animals and things, man and woman were made "in his likeness and image." Mankind was like God, godlike, gifted with attributes far above the abilities of beasts, though not perfect in power and knowledge.

In time the Judeo-Christian anthropology merged with the complementary Greek vision of mankind. According to the Greek thinkers man is someone who lives mentally as well as physically. He comprehends the world by enveloping all things with thought and language, with the *Logos*. Man is free and therefore morally responsible, which means that he can also be immorally irresponsible. He chooses his life "as the archer chooses his target," says Aristotle. He may be good or bad, happy or sad, and he desires to go on living forever.

Endowed with intelligence, speech, and understanding,

and given supervisory responsibility for the earth, man is able to respond to the Divine Persons. Furthermore, God knows him by name and lovingly desires that he live forever. Although he deserved to die for his transgression, the first man knew—as we do still—that he was not meant for death.

In the *Genesis* account of their transgression, it appears that Adam and Eve were not condemned for their new godlike knowledge—"the man is become as one of us"—but punished for the disobedient way they acquired it. At that point innocent, immature Adam and Eve were not prepared to handle good or evil—either can consume the unready— and the proof was the increasingly corrupt generations that followed them. We must remember that they were adults without the lessons of childhood and the example and counseling of parents. It seems that the prohibition was intended for their welfare and we can speculate that perhaps in due time would have been removed as their understanding grew. We could compare them to adolescents who wreak havoc by learning adult ways too soon. But because Adam and Eve disobeyed, sinfulness and suffering became their real condition, everlasting life their true destiny. This remains the tragedy and hope of humanity.

*Genesis* pulsates with primal meanings, which in this context either we must omit altogether or acknowledge only in passing. For example, mankind's imperfect Edenic condition has always been understood negatively to indicate human limitation in contrast to the infinite power and mind of the Creator. But without denying the traditional interpretation, can we not also understand it to mean that unlike an animal, a tiger for instance, which, according to the *Genesis* account, from the beginning is fully perfected in its tigerish being, mankind possesses a mysteriously superior form of being called potentiality and thus is susceptible to perfectibility? A tiger is forever a tiger, but to be human is always to be capable of becoming more so. Or less. The first couple could not have fallen into sin unless they also had the ability to ascend towards higher being. A tiger can do neither.

What the Serpent told Eve was partially right. After the couple had partaken of the forbidden fruit, they were indeed able to discern good and evil just as the Serpent had said and as God himself then declares in *Genesis* 3:22. From this primal human experience we see that we remain susceptible to evil not because it is openly evil but because it contains enough truth to disguise its malice. Satan after all was not demonic in origin but an angelic being who remembered truth even though he was now its enemy.

Concerned that the couple would partake of the Tree of Life and live forever as sinful persons, God hastened to expel them from Eden before the idea occurred to them. It is surprising that we find no previous divine prohibition against consuming the immortalizing fruit. Can we deduce, therefore, that until they sinned the Tree of Life was not forbidden and that they could have eaten of its fruit without punishment or prohibition? Here we see another consequence of evil: it lures us to a smaller good to keep us from a greater one. As for the expulsion itself, the divine motives seems clear enough: as immortal but corrupted persons Adam and Eve would have multiplied evil to unimaginable proportions, surpassing in wickedness even the long-lived antediluvian generations whose obsession was "only evil continually."

An impulsive question occurs to us. Why did God not abolish and undo with a word the evil already loosed in the world by humanity's first transgression? But God is not impulsive. From everything we know of his character it seems that he does not condemn his creation. Else why would He suffer Satan to live or the degenerate human race to survive the disaster of Eden and the Noachian Flood? His character begins to reveal itself in *Genesis*: acting out of love, he prefers to redeem humanity rather than demolish it, and instead of simply abolishing evil by annihilating the evil ones, he chooses to convert their works to good. Instead of destruction he promises Shiloh. What greater proof of the

Divine superiority, and from our perspective what greater punishment for the Enemy, than to discover in the end that all his vile strategies have but served God's higher purposes and that he, the master of evil, has been the servant of greater good?

With few exceptions, orthodox varieties of Christianity hold that in one state or another every human life, though it pass through death, shall live again forever. Death is truly our second birth—to immortal life or unending living death. Viewed from this angle, many Christians think it is wrong to delay the second life by resorting to draconian means to prolong our first, and there are even occasional monstrous extremists who would slaughter children before they fall into sin and thus jeopardize their heavenly chances.

Probably some varieties of Christianity give the Enemy too much credit by declaring that the corruption of mankind ends in sheer personal depravity ("from head to foot," says Calvin). If so, then how can we account for the noble works, enlightened philosophies, and unsurpassed aesthetic creations of pagan Greeks, the engineering feats and governing genius of unredeemed Romans, the development of the alphabet by Baal-worshipping Phoenicians, or the beautiful prehistoric art in the caves of Lascaux and Altamira? How could depraved and giftless men build the pyramids of Egypt and Mexico or stretch out the Great Wall of China? Is it not more reasonable to conclude on the basis of the evidence that although much human giftedness was lost in Eden, much remained, enough for divine Grace to activate it to its purposes? Is it not a form of heresy to think so little of God's supreme creative handiwork as to presume that with a single fell stroke Satan reduced humanity to worthless wretchedness? Is God so easily mocked?

The skeptics ask, where was Eden? The Bible declares in a bare sketch, "And the Lord God planted a garden eastward in Eden; and there he put the man whom he had formed" (*Genesis* 2:8). From the sparse biblical account we can ponder several thoughts as pure speculations. First, the writer of *Genesis* must have had some traditional knowledge or legend about Eden, else there would have been an authorial need to explain the account in greater detail. Second, for Eden to be to his east his reference point must have been west of its remembered site, probably indicating that the *Genesis* account was written after the Hebrews emigrated from Mesopotamia. Third, the garden was divinely designed for mankind and therefore excelled over general creation in due proportion to the excellent status of pre-transgression humanity. Lastly, this divine excellence, the fact that neither Adam nor his descendants ever tried to approach Eden again, and that it is nowhere on earth today not only point to a geographical expulsion but also suggest a simultaneous lowering of the human condition as well. If so, does it mean that Eden and earliest mankind dwelt in a dimension higher than our own and thus was invisible to unaided vision, a plane of human immortality and direct communion with God? Many cultures preserve similar legends of a golden age, extreme human longevity, and a lost demiurgic superiority of mankind.

Scoffers point to parallels between the biblical accounts of the paradisiacal Garden and the Great Flood and similar pagan legends as proof that the Bible itself incorporated these myths. But in truth this argument more readily undermines than supports the skeptical thesis. The nearly universal belief in a Golden Age and traditions of a devastating flood that spared only a few survivors are less likely to be coincidental mythology than corroborative evidence of a universally remembered human catastrophe.

Did Adam and Eve worship God in Eden? Apparently not, at least not as we understand worship today. The Bible states that men began to worship God in the third generation, in the days of Enos, after the expulsion. Neither is there any account of Adam and Eve praying. And no wonder, for at first, God spoke to them directly and sometimes appeared personally in Eden. Elsewhere the Bible states categorically that no man has ever seen God, yet in Eden at least his presence—was it the Pre-incarnate Christ?—was unmistakable and his voice, resoundingly and accusingly clear.

✝✝✝

## 16. Edenic Life and Human Beauty

Following Adam's awkward but glowing approval of the newly created Eve, the unidentified speaker—presumably God Himself—converts the matrimonial event into an imperative: "Therefore shall a man leave his father and his mother and shall cleave unto his wife: and they shall become one flesh" (*Genesis* 2:24). Of course Adam does not yet know Eve personally or sexually. But what may not be as apparent at first is that in his inexperienced innocence neither does he know himself. In coming to know Eve as a woman Adam also comes to realize himself as a man.

The bonds of husband and wife are stronger than the natural ties to parents and family, as the passage makes clear, and for good reason. Parental love protects the child but inhibits the adult. The fledgling does not fly until it leaves the parental nest. For parents there is always a moment of surprise when children emerge into adulthood and reveal their adult character. And children often have a similar experience when they come to know the persons who formerly were only their parents.

The context implies, therefore, that man and woman come to know themselves by knowing each other. They are no longer two but two that are part of one. This means that each sex is defined by its relationship to the other, as our left hand is defined by our right. The poet Antonio Machado wrote that a man is not a man until he hears his name pronounced from the lips of a beautiful woman, and in nearly all older societies a woman was not considered to be fully a woman until she had loved a man.

Probably the aesthetic categories of form, elegance, symmetry, proportion, and harmony are lingering reminders of humanity's original unclothed beauty. For if mankind was God's creative masterpiece, then it makes sense to suppose that the human person was the primary model and focus of our aesthetic sense, which was later abstracted, transmuted,

THE LIGHT OF EDEN

and transferred to other realities. No wonder the nude human body has always been the ideal aesthetic object. "Man," says Protagoras, "is the measure of all things." How much truer this would have been of the first unblemished man and woman. Aristotle wrote that men desire to procreate in beauty, to which we could add that it also stirs them to create in many other ways. Nothing renders us more godlike than the proper expression of this creative desire, and few things defile our humanity more than its perversion.

✝ ✝ ✝

## 17. Nudity, Incest, and Ugliness

Following their transgression Adam and Eve become aware of their nakedness, which in the biblical context we must assume was also nudity. And the proximity of the two experiences may suggest an answer to one of humanity's oldest enigmas: why do people wear clothes? This common practice is one of humanity's most mysterious characteristics, and many theories have been put forth to explain our strange sartorial habits. One ready extra-biblical explanation is that we dress to protect ourselves from inclement weather. Obviously this is so in many instances, yet the Fuegueans of extreme southern South America braved the harshest Antarctic rigors in the nude. On the other hand, the North African Tuaregs cover themselves almost totally, while other people in the same geographical latitudes go about nude, or nearly so.

Others, among them Alphonse the Wise, have suggested that the sense of nudity arose when Adam and Eve saw that unlike themselves, animals were born with fur. Clothing themselves was thus a way of overcoming the perceived advantage animals had over humans. But this theory does not fully account for their shame and does not explain why

Adam and Eve hid from God after their disobedience. We must look elsewhere for a more satisfactory explanation.

As children have always done, they ran away from the scene of their mischief to avoid punishment. But the question of nudity and shame in the Genesis account also hints of a deeper human anguish. Did Adam and Eve become "aware" of their bodies—and hence their nakedness—because already they were beginning to show signs of mortal decay—the "death" about which God had forewarned them and Satan had denied—and therefore were grieved to reveal their spreading blemishes before their Maker? Furthermore, when original sin replaced original innocence the intimacy that nakedness presupposed also was obviously diminished. Clothing has always been a visible admission that people cannot reveal themselves to one another totally in ordinary circumstances. Reserve and psychological barriers were born with self-awareness, and intimacy normally requires extraordinary preparation and exceptional levels of trust.

Physical modesty increases proportionally as the ravages of life and time become more pronounced in our bodies. It is a grave intrusion of privacy to undress the elderly or surprise them in the nude. Ham looked upon his aged father Noah's nakedness, and his descendants were cursed because of it. On the other hand, perhaps one reason why we adore infants is because the cumulative erosions of sin have not yet, or not completely, blemished their primordial beauty. The paradisiacal innocence in infants negates any shame of their nakedness. An undressed infant is not really embarrassingly nude in the same way an adult can be. Its soft round form is itself a covering, and its cherubic body distresses no one, least of all itself. Does not a baby recapitulate the early splendor of Eden and are we not moved to aesthetic delight by its unashamed, innocent perfection?

If clothing was at first a reaction to embarrassment and a mere covering for the nude human body, it soon acquired the quality of aesthetic enhancement. The visibility or superficiality of the first men—and certain primitives today—gave way to the characteristics of privacy, conceal-ment, and personal depth. Shame yielded to its gentler cousin, modesty. Between the primitive covering God provided Adam and Eve in Eden and Joseph's gaudy "coat of many colors" an "aesthetic of attire" obviously had devel-oped and with it an entirely new dimension of human reality.

Clothing reveals by partially concealing and suggests without fully revealing. If the nude human body was the first aesthetic focus, the clad body was likely the first artistic creation. By our style of dress we work a daily artistry on our body. Clothing is a work of art in a double sense: as a suggestive art of the body and as an artistic creation itself. But as with most art, its higher dimensions involve respon-sive human imagination. In itself a work of art amounts to very little. The greatest art arouses almost no aesthetic response in brutish people, and none at all in animals. Only when human imagination extends it to its suggestive limits do the creative features of dress approach completion. This "aesthetic of attire" functions only under the stimulation of imagination. With a line, a color, a combination, a move-ment, the imagination begins its creative flight and does not stop until it has completed its ideal enhancement of the concealed body. But the body so conceived is not the natural body of a person but an aesthetic creation and experience. A person so perceived is not confined to nature but raised to a more appealing form in the imagination. The natural body leaves very little to the imagination, the aesthetically clothed body, almost everything. But this is a gain, not a loss, for imagination soars above and beyond nature, taking what it offers and reworking it into a more beautiful state.

In its natural and nude state the human body is surpris-ingly impersonal and correspondingly unappealing, which causes us to suspect that personal beauty becomes so only when it is first imagined. We are humanized by imagina-tion, and to the degree that we diminish its prestige and deny its place we reduce our humanity. Those who live by facts alone subsist on a beggar's diet.

Clothing is also a form of insertion in society. By our dress and attire we not only proclaim our allegiance to a certain era and generation but also reveal our personal measure of obedience or departure from its norms. "Clothes make the man," the old saying goes, to which we could add: they also unmake him. Today the notion has fallen into disrepute, for we like to think the person we are is previous and impervious to the way we dress. In exceptional cases, this may be so, but in most our attire is a reliable predictor of who we are. It is a proclamation of where we are in life and how much we are in accord or at cross purposes with the world. Clothes speak to our vision of life; they are our daily personal headline.

If the first humans were genetically and aesthetically perfect, or nearly so, then the modern prohibitions against incest would have been unnecessary. Indeed, we do not find them in the earliest biblical accounts. The Ten Commandments, for instance, do not include an eleventh forbidding incest. As late as the last Patriarchs, men were still marrying their close relatives, in Abraham's case, his half-sister Sarah. In order to preserve family purity, generations of Pharaohs, Incas, and other royal lines married their full blood sisters. The question skeptics often raise about the spouses of Adam's children leads to an obvious answer: they surely married their siblings and cousins, and apparently they did so without social onus or taboo. Long ages of increasing genetic deterioration passed before prohibitions against incest were instituted in nearly all human cultures.

If aesthetic sensitivity is a reminder of our divine origin and beauty—its sign, then it suggests that what may be called "the cult of ugliness," which in recent times has been infesting art, music, literature, speech, dress, manners, worship, and other dimensions of modern life, degrades our humanity and mocks our Creator. Today we barely protest its aggressive advances. Most of us either fear accusations of artistic or social boorishness or we have lived so long with ugliness and mediocrity that we neither demand nor appreciate excellence.

The phantom psychic tremor we experience in the presence of ugliness has all but replaced genuine aesthetic emotion. The ideal of modern art and literature seems to be an ugly theme beautifully or skillfully treated. But would it not be preferable to begin with a beautiful subject and by treating it beautifully produce a doubly beautiful work? This was the supposition of Classic art, and as far as I know, though often rejected it has never been surpassed.

By way of a Christian rebuttal to my argument, we are told that beauty is in the eye of the beholder and that God Himself looks at the heart, not the outward appearance. This may be true, yet the Bible hints that physical beauty is not a matter of indifference but is itself a gift. God created the face as well as the heart, and neither was ugly to begin with. In any case, confronted with ugliness, especially human ugliness, we experience the involuntary psychic shudder just mentioned and long since socially controlled, as though we were seeing something that was never meant to be. And no wonder; by definition ugliness is alien to creation and proof that something has gone wrong. In its presence we experience a momentary disappointment of hope. And we can guess the cause: beauty is our divine expectation and ugliness its visible contradiction. We could not recognize ugliness at all if first we did not have a notion of beauty.

But are there really recognizable norms of beauty and ugliness? We have heard the old argument that aesthetic perceptions are simply learned as a function of culture or that they can be reduced to evolutionary survival values. Cultural nuances do exist, and certainly God looks at what is in our heart, yet none of the arguments impugn the fact that every race and culture has a native aesthetic sense, which is then susceptible to local modification.

Perhaps we perceive beauty in the same or similar way we recognize truth. Both resonate to our deeper nature as though we were created to receive and respond to them, as though we were destined from the start for truth and beauty. And no wonder; the Master's sheep know their shepherd's voice, which is always a message of perfect truth and beauty, and no other will they heed regardless of how alluring or seductive it may be.

Within this context probably the most pervasive pedagogical problem of our time is the vast amount of untruth, unredemptive truth, and immoral ugliness we try to teach the young. But the young, like the old, are not so easily duped as we think. Regardless of its disguises, we perceive untruth in a manner fundamentally different from the way truth affects us, just as beauty and ugliness can never be truly made to pass for each other. In rude ways students show their rejection of false theories, erroneous hypotheses, errant facts, crypto-political agendas, and dehumanizing conclusions by their invincible inattentiveness and alarming disrespect for schools and teachers. Despite every lure and incentive we can think of to encourage them, they refuse to learn what we ought not to teach them in the first place. We hear that information multiplies exponentially every few years, but does anyone know how much of this so-called information is really misinformation or worse, disinformation?

It makes sense that truth strikes us from a different angle and stirs in us a different response from falsehood. As Christians we hold that we were created in truth and for truth, and only in truth can we be fulfilled. As we saw earlier, evil seduces only insofar as it can disguise itself as good. But let us be truthful about truth. For many generations it has had a bad press and a depressing image of confession, contrition, austerity, and grim self-denial. It smacks of desperation and the failure of more alluring things. The perception persists that truth is something we embrace on the failing, downward slopes of life. We fall back on truth only when we have fallen on our face and have no happier option.

Nothing could be further from truth than these dreary images inherited from cheerless strains of both Protestantism and Catholicism. The truth of Eden was exuberant, matutinal, creative, beaming and brimming with happiness, the happiness that God Himself expressed when he looked on his creation and was pleased with his work.

Wickedness, which perennially enjoys a good press, forever promises happiness, but it always delivers misery instead. For if it were not so then evildoers themselves would not fear the fruits of evil. Evil always fails as those who accept its Machiavellian lures always fail; most of all they fail to be themselves, which is the primal failure. Until we live in the truth we are always somebody else and never anybody we truly admire.

✝✝✝

## 18. Named and Nameless

The defining reciprocity between the sexes means that Adam and Eve—and all the generations after them—did not live together in simple parity or equality but in a state of dynamic, disjunctive equilibrium subject to the characteristic shifts and readjustments of living human reality. The sexes are different but inseparably different. Whatever affects one sex necessarily affects the other, for each is mirrored and defined in the other. Sexual union is, or may be, a component of their relationship, but it is only one of several others that I choose to describe as "sexuate." An infant is not sexually active yet is subject to sexuate distinctions from the day it is born: blue for boys, pink for girls, etc. Likewise, the very elderly or the celibate do not engage in sexual activities but obviously retain their sexuate identity as men and women. In summary, one must be sexuate in order to be sexual, but one may be sexuate without being sexual.

God Himself declared in *Genesis* what human experience has confirmed ever since: that it is not good for man to be alone, and for that reason in the strangest of procedures packed with symbolic meanings he created a "help-meet" for Adam, Eve, or *Khavvaw* ("life"). With characteristic male absorption in external matters, Adam was busied with his chores in Eden: naming the creatures, supervising the garden, and so forth. Nevertheless, it was not lost on Adam, and certainly not on God, that while every creature had its mate, he was alone. Yet without divine help, his longing would have remained nameless and unfocused, for he had no image of woman. He longed for whom he had never known; his desire was inexpressible, like color to the blind or music to the deaf. It is a longing echoed to one degree or another in the life of every person until they find their beloved.

In his euphoric delight at seeing his new help-meet for the first time, Adam first identified her generically as woman (*Ishá*) because she was taken from man (*Ish*). But after this play on the Hebrew words, he then named her Eve, which was also a description in the Semitic manner, for as he remarked, she was, or was to be, the "mother of all living," except of course for Adam himself, we are tempted to point out to the biblical writer. But then on second thought perhaps he also should be included and even made foremost among those to whom she gave life. For until he met and loved her, Adam did not really begin to live a manly, humanized life. Only by identifying the woman as feminine Eve could the creature Adam begin to understand himself the man Adam.

Although from Adam to Abraham men had no family names that we know of—and still have nonesuch in some cultures—from the first, human persons bore proper names, unlike the generic names which, at God's instigation and to his curiosity, Adam gave the other creatures of Eden. But why was this vocative and nominative task entrusted to Adam in the first place? Naturally we cannot know for sure, but having placed the world at man's disposal, does it not make sense that God would allow him to humanize it with names, and by doing so, to obey the divine command to take responsibility for it? For at a primary level to be able to name a thing is a way of taking possession of it. It is the first step in ownership of reality.

To bear a proper human name is also the first indication that with persons we are confronted with a reality unlike any other. Personal names are the first stage of anthropological metaphysics, that is, the reality of the human person. Yet according to modern thought human reality is "derivative," which means that in theory it can be understood genetically, equated to other animal species, and, ultimately, reduced to biological and chemical components. For a long time it was hoped—quite logically, it must be admitted—that by reversing the process and recombining these organic components under controlled conditions we could create life. The logic was clear enough but the experiments always failed. Why? Obviously the technique was inadequate and probably the hypothesis was simplistically flawed.

For this reason we can accept certain facts of this assumption while discarding the assumption itself. We grant, for example, that *what* a child's physical body is derives from parents and ancestors and shows a close physical kinship to other mammalian species, especially the higher primates. But in order to know *who* the child is we must think in an entirely different way, beginning with the acknowledgment of a personal name that distinguishes the child from all others. This remains true even with individuals bearing the same name. *What* a child is has genetic, zoological, and chemical antecedents; it may resemble family members in certain traits and character and like many animals it has a spine, a head, two eyes, two ears, one mouth, teeth, internal organs, and five digits on each of its four limbs. But *who* the child is and may become cannot be reduced to anything beyond or previous to itself. In the truest sense, it is what all loving parents know in their hearts: a new creation, inseparable from its ancestors yet irreducible to them.

A name is not a definition, as we define a square, a pentagon, or the tiger we met earlier, but an acknowledgment of human life's internal propriety, its proper being or intimacy. In no way should we mistake this intimate personal reality for the unchanging essence or inner substance of things that philosophers sought for more than two thousand years. For as we saw earlier, unlike other realities human life is always in a process of becoming more or less than itself. And the desirable state is to become who we were meant to be in the beginning: the image and likeness of God.

In our diminished Christianity and excessive humbleness this seems too lofty an aim for mere mortals, and we are prone to view it as hubris and heresy. Yet Jesus said plainly to his disciples, "Be ye therefore perfect, even as your Father which is in heaven is perfect" (*Matthew*: 5:48). For their part, the ancient Greeks wisely reserved judgment about a person's life and happiness until it was mortally ended, for until death human life is subject to creative alteration or destructive negation.

Unlike other living beings, human life possesses imponderable depths. There is vastly more on the inside of life than outside—and the outside, the exterior world, is also humanly interiorized, as we shall see in a later chapter. Every human life is a universe, and as Unamuno once said in a moment of bizarre inspiration, every person of flesh and blood is worth more than the whole material universe. This is why personal life is essentially modest, revealing but also concealing a world of potentiality unto itself, a world capable of enrichment or impoverishment. The name we call another, as Adam named Eve, is our primary acknowledgment of that person's inner mystery and deep reality.

✝✝✝

## 19. Loving Eve and Facing the World

In its highest form this interiority may admit intimate relationships of love or friendship. Adam "knew" Eve sexually; he discovered or uncovered her in an intimate relationship, but he did not and could not know her totally in that single union. Every act of true intimacy is a further experience of another person's mystery. Lovers discover each other in intimacy, and they go on discovering each other throughout their life. For human life is not simply given once and for all time but is always coming into being, always being revealed, yet because of its depth always partially concealed. To love another person is to be embarked on a journey of mutual discovery that lasts throughout life in this world—and, who knows?—perhaps in higher ways in the next as well. A mark of true love is the inexhaustible enthusiasm one has for the familiar mystery— if I may use the paradoxical term—of the beloved.

Everyday language has never been misled by problematic modern thinking. When someone knocks on our door, we do not ask "*what's* there?" but "*who* is it?" For if that person were to respond, "A member of the species *homo sapiens sapiens,*" we would dismiss the information as an absurdity, for despite its scientific accuracy it tells us next to nothing about the identity, or "self-sameness," of the caller at our door. On the other hand, if the caller answers "Tom" or "Sue" then a whole biographical panorama opens up; we recognize a person—perhaps a friend, a relative, an acquaintance, a rival, an enemy—but not an unnamed biological animal. In the Scriptures the Lord insists many times on the hallowedness of his Name. And they assure us that God will call us by name also, perhaps by a name that is even more intimate and meaningful than the one we bear in this life, for only God truly knows us and calls us by our true name. In this world human reality is not primarily biological but biographical, and a human name is an abbreviated biography. So is a tombstone.

Because it is characterized by depth, intimacy, and concealment human life becomes known to us as expression, as an exteriorization of itself. This occurs in two primary modes: verbal and facial.

Even though surely he had spoken earlier when he named the creatures of Eden, Adam's first recorded words were uttered in wonderment and love when he first saw

Eve. "This is now bone of my bones, and flesh of my flesh" (*Genesis* 2:23). In the first case, Adam utters the sense, or meaning, of his Edenic world, as we try to make sense of ours before love transforms our life. By doing so he is able to categorize and assume a certain intellectual mastery of the creatures God presents to him. But in the second case, in Eve's presence, we discern an added dimension to this bare nomenclature. Adam not only sees and names Eve but takes the further step of expressing—and most likely discovering—his personal and masculine sensations that her presence arouses.

From this moment forward Adam makes no recorded reference to his former life, probably because his real life starts when he begins to love Eve. It is the age-old experience of lovers; former things fade like a dream and the beloved so fills their life that it seems they have always known each other yet will never tire of knowing each other more fully. No wonder Adam's verbalized astonishment—and ours for that matter—occurs in an amorous or "lovely" encounter, for he was created by God out of love, and God is love, the cosmic love that contains inchoately all the forms that love may take in human experience.

The Bible tells us that God spoke the worlds into being. Christians believe that the Creative, Eternal Word, the *Logos* of St. John's Gospel, was Christ himself and that "All things were made by him . . ." (*St. John* 1:3). Language is a divine gift. We admit that words have power, but it would be more accurate to say that they are power. And as a divine gift from the source of truth and beauty, they were meant to express these sacred qualities. In the short term, probably nothing illustrates better than language the fall of mankind from a higher state of grace. For if language was a divine gift meant to express the power of truth and beauty, divided human languages were a curse that became the first and greatest barriers to understanding. Not only this, but in their perverted state words readily serve the cause of ugliness, division, and untruth. And the more we use them in this way, even in prayer and devotion, the less powerful and expressive they become.

His solitary sojourn in Eden thus ended, Adam found himself face to face with Eve, as men and women, friends and family members, strangers and beloved persons have faced one another ever since. Adam's encounter with wondrous Eve was not an episodic interlude but the beginning of their life together in a forward, futuristic manner. Together they "face" the world.

We can say that the human face is the physical correlate of the temporal forwardness and verbal expressiveness of human life. In this sense it is both noun and verb. We "face" the future and in turn our vision of the future configures our face. Beneath our racial and cultural traits the vision of life we pursue and what happens to us as we do—our purpose or purposelessness in this world, our honesty or deception, our mental alertness or dullness, happiness or pain, joy or sorrow—molds our face into its image. We inherit certain genetic and generic facial characteristics, but by about age forty we can no longer conceal who we have become; our face has become our autobiography. Abraham Lincoln once made the disquieting statement that after age forty we are responsible for our face. Over time it becomes the blueprint of our life.

This is why true lovers never tire of staring at the beloved's face, especially the eyes, and, like Adam, praising the beloved's beauty. For what lovers do most is look and talk, both of which are facially centered. The body is erotic and thus the focus of those engaged in physical eroticism, but the human face is maximally erogenous and expressive of personal love and life.

We cannot say that a woman is beautiful or a man handsome, without reference to their face. A faceless human torso is disturbingly impersonal, much like a mannequin, and an expressionless face on an otherwise handsome body seems to nullify its graces and disappoint our aesthetic expectations. Biology is diffused throughout the body, but personhood is concentrated in the face. We could say that it is the visible metaphor of life's frontal, futuristic mission.

Naturally many faces are not beautiful or handsome, and

some women make no attempt to beautify themselves. In that negligence she ceases to function as woman and denies her feminine condition. But must woman be beautiful to fulfill her role? No, certainly not, but in order to be woman, she must try to be beautiful, that is, as beautiful as she can be, just as man must try to be strong, as strong as he can be, even though nature and circumstances have not endowed him with great physical power or means. We are never fully ourselves, never fully beautiful, never really strong in this world, yet it is a betrayal of our condition not to make the effort to be.

If we expect to find beauty in a woman's face or the grace that suggests it and often functions as its stand-in, what do we look for in a masculine countenance? We need to preface our answer by reminding ourselves that human life is needy, indigent, and incomplete, subject to mortality and ignorance. In a word, man is weak. Throughout the ages he has envied the greater power of animals and forever tried to imitate them. For man's aim is the very opposite of weakness: knowledge, strength, assurance, and power. Adam was responsible for the Garden, and man in his manhood has not ceased to be, or at least to feel, responsible for his world.

Is man, therefore, a mere imposter in his pretense to power? Some varieties of modern psychology and feminist theories subscribe to this subversive interpretation of men. But it is important to distinguish between claiming to possess these attributes and aiming for them. The honest man knows that he is not fully any of the things he aims for—otherwise he would not have to aim for them to start with. But in order to be a man at all he must try to be who he has not yet become, and indeed may never become. Therefore, his manliness, indeed his manhood, is measurable less by what he is than by who he tries to be. This is why human life is futuristic and why courage traditionally has ranked first in the worldly inventory of masculine virtues. It is a peculiarly human characteristic born out of vulnerability and weakness. Only if we fear can we be courageous. The indestructible gods were not privileged to know bravery.

Just as the face reveals the character of human life, it also conceals its depths. Etymologically "person"—*persona*, or *prosopon* (face) in Greek—means "that which sounds through" (*per*=through + *sonare*=to sound), and it refers in the first instance to Classical actors speaking through the comic and tragic masks they wore on stage. But the recent reemergence in the English language of the Latin word *persona* as an exterior or public personality is even more significant. Our persona is the dimension of ourselves we reveal in order to conceal the more intimate person we are. Ironically the face, which reveals the most, also conceals the most about us.

What do we see in the masculine face? To begin with, not the same beauty or its graceful substitute we expect to find in the feminine face. For this reason most languages, including English, have different words to indicate feminine beauty and male handsomeness. Indeed, feminine beauty in a male face is disturbing, and we scarcely know what to make of it. Unless the male face denotes a failed or frivolous life—for I repeat that human life admits of degrees—we find first of all a quality we could call the weight or seriousness of life, what the ancient Romans called *gravitas*. Behind his physical handsomeness or ugliness, his age and racial imprint, a man's face reveals the seriousness of life and the way he has come to grips with it. *Gravitas* in man corresponds to grace in woman.

Woman is lighter of body and features than man and is less prone to the cruder forces that harden man's life. This is why men find verbal or physical grossness in women to be especially repugnant. As *Genesis* tells us, and men condescendingly repeat, she was a further refinement of Adam's cruder clay. This airiness and softness combine to produce her alluring, elusive mystery that perplexes and provokes man. She attracts man, sets him in motion, and draws him out of his customary masculine taciturnity. She is provocative, as Eve provoked Adam to utter what amounted to a primeval lyric outpouring over her beauty. The first man was the first poet. And so it has always been: as Plato said, when love touches us we turn poetic.

Woman's provocative, elusive beauty arouses in man a hint of ontological distress. Adam was absorbed in the care of the Garden until Eve appeared to inspire in him a greater care. Her fugitive, evasive charms promise to rapture him out of his laborious responsibilities and turn his life toward happiness, but this wonderful possibility may also elude him unless he acts quickly and boldly to claim her before she slips away. This is why for the man in love hope and despair, courage and fear, daring and doubt never stand far apart.

Yet this fanciful view of the initial phase of love in men and women is but one dimension of their disjunctive, reciprocal, and ever-changing relationship. If woman is hard to get, she is harder to lose—if she is interested and he is interesting. She is never so elusive that he cannot overtake her if she wishes and if he has the manly determination to persist. In older language man becomes the "suitor," which in its original Latin root means "follower" or "pursuer."

Beyond their mutual pursuit and reciprocal capture, however, men and women reveal very different and even paradoxical reactions to their amorous situation. Man who lives with his feet planted on the ground and the weight of the world on his shoulders—every serious man shares the burden of Atlas—also has another side to his being. Far horizons beckon to him; he is afflicted with an ontological and geographical wanderlust. He is planted here but dreams also of elsewhere. Woman's love provokes man to action and stirs him to ambition. But then her fear is that he may not stop when she does, that her charms may not be able to hold him to home, hearth, and family. Perhaps this is why woman often fears man's greater ambitions and urges compromise and security over lofty, risky achievement.

Facing Eve for the first time Adam declares that she is now a part of his very being. She was taken from his body in God's strange surgical procedure, but in a much more profound and personal way now she comes back into his life to complete it. He gave her being and now receives her unto himself so that his own being may be complete. By his jolting admission we see that this encounter was not a mere erotic interlude, not a momentary experience, not something he did with Eve, but a new state of being. He needed Eve but not in the same way he needed food or water. These he needed for his biological being but Eve he needed for his biographical life. He needed her not as woman but as the only woman in order to be the man he was destined to be. Yet because Eve is a person she is always emerging into being, always dynamically coming to be, which means that henceforth they will be embarked on a lifelong relationship of mutual giving and receiving.

To live humanly is to live in anticipation of love, and as every lover and mystic knows, to live fully is to love fully. Since they were created in love, man and woman live out of an original "lovely" predisposition, which can, sadly, be distorted, perverted, and supplanted by imitations. The lover meets our expectations. Of what? Of satisfying our deepest yearning to become our authentic self. Love is always an experience of coming into our own, of being who we really are, of living up to ourselves. From this it follows, as Adam makes clear, that love is irrevocable; the lover becomes "bone of my bone and flesh of my flesh." And we could add, soul of my soul. Even the most miserable of lovers believes his love is worthwhile. He says "yes" to it because to renounce it would be to deny his very life.

Everything human is risky and nothing more so than love. Nothing fails more often, yet nothing is born again with such high expectations. In love we know that we are staking our lives on a gamble, and we may lose. But even if we do we prefer our pain to a loveless life. The world subscribes to what Tennyson said: "Tis better to have loved and lost than never to have loved at all." There are worse fates than a broken heart, among them a life never awakened to love, human or divine.

The world-weary cynic would say that all this has

happened before in unnumbered generations and to countless people, and the elderly would say that they experienced
it all long before. That may be, but it never happened to us,
never personally to me, the "me" that each of us is. Those
who have truly loved cannot be duped by cynicism. Every
lover knows that his love is one of a kind. No real love and
no real person will ever be duplicated. Every love is a first
love. Every love is an only love.

Love is our deepest calling, and in all its authentic forms
its call sounds unto eternity. No lover, and no lover of God,
accepts a love short of forever. Here Christian faith and
human love converge in enhanced hopes of immortality. As
sweethearts, spouses, relatives, parents, children, friends,
and believers we wisely refuse to surrender our loves at the
grave and pronounce them ended with our fragile mortality.
No. Beyond that mortal bourn, struggling with heavy heart
against doubts and the evidence of our eyes, we foresee
what we cannot see: in God's providence no love is lost, no
beauty spent, though time may bring them pause. God
holds all things in trust till we discern their cause. Here is
the core of our Christian faith and the sustaining trust of our
life: those we love shall live again with us and more abun-
dantly so, and if the Bible and the Church teachings be true,
everything good and true and lovely in our life will be
saved, intensified, and reborn with us. And everything shall
be wholly revealed—*Quidquid latet apparebit*—in its full
personal depth and we shall be truly ourselves as God has
called us by name to be. Let us make an even bolder claim:
by faith we glimpse at certain moments a truth that our
imperfect Christian understanding, deficient languages,
and residual paganism will not let us fully comprehend:
though our bodies are mortal and die, there are no dead
people. What I am dies; who I am lives. No one living or
deceased deserves to be consigned only to the past tense.
Everyone who was, is, and shall forever be.

At the end of earthly life human love and Christian faith
converge in hope for the believer and anguish for the unbeliever. For if there is no hope for tomorrow, then there is

really none for today either. The unbeliever's life is contradicted by death and his love blasphemed by mortality. To believe that life has no immortal meaning is to be convinced that it also lacks mortal meaning. For the Christian the contrary is true: the eve of his joy is already joyful; he can be happy today because he knows he will be happier tomorrow. As the dawning sun banishes the shades of night long before it breaks over the horizon, so we anticipate approaching happiness with a glad vesper.

✝✝✝

## 20. Too Good to be True?

All that we have seen so far—and we have barely touched the surface—converges in a Christian understanding of human reality that is incomparably more respectful and edifying of the human person than any other vision of mankind. This Christian perspective, itself enriched by excellent Hebrew and Greek antecedents, elevates mankind to an unparalleled dignity as the supreme earthly creation of God and the beneficiary of a magnificent inheritance in the next world. And in this world it stimulated forms of governance, ethics, art, learning, charity, benevolence, law, brotherhood, and progress which if not completely unique at least are unequaled by any competing anthropology.

So wonderful indeed was this Christian perspective of mankind that beginning around the time of the Reformation and accelerating in the Enlightenment, many people thought it was simply too good to be true. Paradoxically, the more willful and insubordinate men became in the age of Reformation the more certain religious reformers came to believe that mankind lacked free will. And the more human knowledge expanded with the emerging new sciences the dimmer the view some men took of humanity. From these queer tendencies two anthropologies, one neo-Christian and the other scientific, emerged to compete with the traditional view that had prevailed for over a millennium and a half. Consider each in turn.

John Calvin (1509-1564) argued against free will and for the odd combination of predestination, human depravity, irresistible grace, and selective salvation. And in Catholic realms Cornelius Jansenius (1585-1638) made similar arguments for "invincible grace" and took a Calvinesque view of hopeless human depravity. Jansenism, which had many adherents in France and the Low Countries and counted no less a luminary than Blaise Pascal among its adherents, after a fierce struggle with the Catholic Magisterium was confined eventually to its last stronghold in the abbey of Port-Royal in France where it was finally abolished, at least nominally, its adherents scattered, and its buildings razed.

On the other hand, Calvinism, sometimes called Augustinianism after St. Augustine of Hippo, continued to strengthen under the likes of Theodore Beza, John Knox, John Bunyan, Jonathan Edwards, Charles Spurgeon, and, in modified form, Karl Barth and Francis Schaeffer. Today all or parts of it are entrenched as theological doctrine in several Protestant denominations.

We must respect the earnest and gifted minds that have believed, or still believe, in Calvinistic or Jansenistic predestination and related doctrines. And as we have tried to do in other cases, we should try to understand, as far as our knowledge permits, the basis for their theology.

The case for predestination seems straightforward. The most persuasive argument is the unarguable omniscience of God. The Calvinists reasoned that if God knows all, as surely he must to be God, then he must know the future and who will and will not be saved. Done in by total depravity, man can in no wise come to God on his own or work out his own salvation, for his thoughts, like those of antediluvian mankind, are turned continuously to evil. Only the divine intervention of the Holy Spirit can overcome the dreadful wickedness of his soul and turn him willy-nilly to repentance and obedience. American preacher Jonathan Edwards called this "The holy rape of the soul." All men deserve death for their transgressions, but God selects some for salvation while leaving others to their deserved damnation. Man, therefore, is neither the author nor the actor of his life but a depraved creature, more a mannequin than a man, whom God may, if he chooses, overwhelm with irresistible grace and place among the elect. At every juncture of human life God alone chooses to act through sinful man or, alternatively, to abandon him to the Hell he has earned.

This means that the sacrificial Christ at Calvary offers only limited atonement. He takes away the Original Sin of the elect but not of all humanity. The unselected continue on their way to perdition in what is sometimes called "double damnation," that is, damned at birth and again at death.

Meanwhile the saints, i.e., the elect, are forever immune to condemnation. Salvation is a gift that can neither be earned nor lost. As the reassuring popular Calvinistic saying goes, "once saved, always saved;" to which we could add its terrifying complement, "and once lost, always lost."

An open question remains in Calvinistic theology itself whether this divine prescience is prescriptive or descriptive, whether by foreknowing our destiny God also determines it. In certain passages (*Romans* 8:29-30, for instance) the Bible appears to lend unequivocal textual support to Calvinistic, Jansenistic, and similar doctrines, but others just as clearly suggest a different interpretation. The Annunciation (*St. Luke* 1:28-38) takes Mary's freedom into account, for her willing acceptance of the Incarnation is essential. In *2 Peter* 3:9 we read that it is not God's will that any should perish, ". . . but that all should come to repentance." There are, of course, dialectical roads around such passages if one makes the determination to search for them, but gratuitous detours often indicate that we have strayed from the right way and are unwilling to admit our error.

The episode of "the rich young ruler" recounted in the Gospels of *Matthew* 19:16-23 and *Mark* 10:17-23 is also particularly puzzling from a Calvinist point of view. Knowing beforehand what his decision would be, why would Jesus tell the young man to give up his possessions and follow him? The setting seems to indicate that the man was free to follow or not. At the time and with great sadness he chose not to follow Jesus, yet we do not know what happened later in his life. Early Church historian Eusebius writes that fifteen bishops "of the circumcision" served in Jerusalem before its destruction and many Jews came to believe. The "young ruler" could have been among them. Who has not resisted the first call to personal authenticity only to yield later to a persistent inner yearning?

But the *Paternoster*, or Lord's Prayer, in words spoken by Jesus himself, may raise the most questions about Calvinist reasoning. Jesus prays that "Thy will be done on earth as it is in heaven." Naturally, we have no doubt that God's will prevails in heaven, as the prayer indicates, but Jesus also asks that it be done on earth, *implying that it is possible for it not to be done.* Yet according to Calvinist doctrine God's will is not only sovereign but already sovereignly exercised always and everywhere, in heaven and on earth, and in the life of every person. If so, then shall we be forced to conclude that Jesus taught his disciples—and us—an idle and futile prayer? And indeed could we not speculate that all petitioning prayer is vain, since God has preordained all things and all people and does not change his ordinances? If Calvin and his followers are right, then the only reason to take the Gospel to the uttermost parts of the earth appears to be because Jesus commanded it, not because it would change the destiny of anyone who hears it.

There are, in summary, many arguments in favor of Calvinism and similar movements over the course of Christianity. Otherwise they would not have gained so many adherents and so many intelligent defenders. But the more one ponders the Calvinistic reasoning, the more circular and self-contradictory it appears to become.

To begin with, Calvinistic reasoning diminishes Christ and the significance of the Cross. His sacrifice did not touch many, perhaps most, of those lost in sin. Do we not, then, end up with a diminished Savior whose sacrifice was

THE LIGHT OF EDEN

perhaps unnecessary to start with? And what can we say to his promise to mankind that "ye shall know the truth and the truth shall set you free" (*John* 8:32)? Would not the Calvinist or Jansenist response to the lost have to be, "Ye shall know the truth and it will condemn you forever?"

Likewise, from a Calvinist and Jansenist standpoint nearly the entire Old Testament becomes a strange exercise in divine futility. From *Genesis* to *Malachi* God warns and exhorts His people to foreswear evil and return to him. The last verse in the King James version of the Old Testament ends with God's final threat: ". . . lest I come and smite the earth with a curse" (*Malachi* 4:6). In *Deuteronomy* 30:19 God plainly states: "I have placed before you life and death, the blessing and the curse; choose life." But for people who lack free will and are hopelessly corrupted by evil, as the Calvinists and Jansenists assert, these divine exhortations would have no effect and God's holy anger would be beside the point. How could he expect a helplessly unrighteous people to repent of their unrighteousness on their own? And what good would it do to berate them for it if there is no chance that they will change their predetermined minds?

But the crowning heresy of Calvinism and similar movements appears to consist of belittling the Creator himself. To deprive his supreme creature of free will and then to overwhelm man with divine omniscience and grace is to reduce the Creator to little more than a gifted maker of preprogrammed automatons.

At the same time, Calvinism ironically exalts and magnifies the destructive work of Satan, as we saw earlier. After Eden it would take God ages to repair the creation that Satan ruined in an instant. And what about the Enemy himself? Was he the only creature left to roam about with free will? Or was he, too, preprogrammed to do what he did? Was he merely God's Devil? The longer we follow the dialectical implications of Calvinism, the more monstrous they become, and despite every precaution, monstrously heretical. Beginning with its inadequate anthropology, a deficient understanding of who man is, we progress inex-

III / *Varieties of Anthropology* 79

orably to an inadequate theology, to a defective knowledge of who God is.

Human freedom is dangerous. For whence comes evil if not from its misuse? Can we not imagine a hushed thrill of expectation and wonderment in the tense celestial cohort as the Creator, having completed the vast preliminary cycles of creation and prepared the world for his masterpiece, now utters the climactic words: "Let us make man in our image, after our likeness . . ." (*Genesis* 1:26). Because it is divine in origin, freedom involves great responsibility and for that reason may result in great irresponsibility. Was the heavenly host apprehensive about what or whom God was about to unleash in the Cosmos? Surely it takes divine love and knowledge to tolerate and sustain freedom. It is even tempting at times to sympathize with those who distrust it and argue against it. At exasperating moments, who has not felt a secret sympathy for tyranny?

These are normal complaints. What does not seem right is for such objections to freedom to bear the name of Christianity, which holds that God has created mankind, men and women, in his likeness and image. Therefore, they are meant to be free, truly free, as Christ said. It takes a great God, much greater than the arbitrary puppet master of Calvinism and Jansenism, to be able to accommodate human freedom.

✝✝✝

## 21. A Greater God?

Reasoning from biblical accounts and Christian theology, we can argue that the God of Christianity does not limit himself to the foreknowledge of our acts. He did not and does not, because of Satan's evil acts, usurp the very system of free chances and choices he made possible for mankind. He did not pull back from his damaged creation or settle for a lesser humanity. Instead he provided that through Christ both would be redeemed and reemerge more glorious than before. Like all those who respect the integrity of persons, God is not a meddler; he does not usurp our privacy or subvert our free will. He is not a heavenly voyeur. His knowledge and power surely must be infinitely greater, or our very salvation is at risk.

Because God is God, more than merely knowing what we will do, which would reduce him to the status of a demiurgic seer or magician, he must know all the possible acts and pathways of happening open to the free will of mankind. More, he is able to adjust and hold in balance the workings of the entire material and moral universe—in time and beyond time as we reckon it—in order to accommodate our actions, our mistakes, our chosen and missed opportunities, our repentance. Physicist Stephen Hawking said we could do the same had we a computer large enough to calculate all the possibilities inherent in quantum mechanics. Surely God's celestial vision is even wider and more responsive. Emerson wrote of the deep remedial power ever at work in the world, and the Bible tells us that God can restore "the years that the locusts have eaten."

For this reason the state or condition we call Heaven is surely a busy, exciting life as the complex workings of the entire cosmos are kept in dynamic balance and on course towards its divine ends and purposes. Those who expect a placid eternity of perpetual rest or of endless harping and hymning probably have their sights set on a lesser Heaven. Indeed, an eternity with nothing creative to do would bear an ominous resemblance to Hell.

One problem is that we have given less thought to the glory of Heaven than to the gore of Hell. We have thought of it in the main as a reward for righteous living in this world, as a prize for a race well run and a fight well fought, as the calm and the balm after the storm and stress of this life. And there on this happy note the story of human life climaxes and ends. Or does it? Perhaps we would do better to think of Heaven more dynamically as the opportunity not merely to rest forever from a concluded life in this world but to commence a fully personal life in the presence of the fully personal God. Contemplated in this way, Heaven is not the conclusion of the human story but its true beginning.

Human freedom in this world reflects already this cosmic openness and adjustment; at any moment, countless ways are open to us, and each of them has universal implications. Every human act alters the world for good or ill. By our lives and actions we affect the protean shaping of creation.

Enlightenment philosopher David Hume claimed to have disconnected material cause and effect, as his generation of thinkers sought to disengage human actions from moral accountability. In a more responsible doctrine of consequences, however, we see that there are no random acts and none without effect. As the poet Donne reminds us, no man is an island. To which we might add, for every person is a continent. Hence the immeasurable consequences of our prayers, love, charity, and well-done deeds. The world is much more durable and responsive than our pessimists fear, and much more accountable and punitive than our immoralists dream. This is why it survives doomsayers and catastrophes. The unfailing dawning of each day and the firm earth under our feet are abiding proof of the essential integrity of God's world. Creation was damaged but not doomed by humanity's primal sins. As the poet Jorge Guillén said, the world is well made. And there is a divine plan to make it even better.

If we are predestined, as the Calvinists, Jansenists, and other Christians of similar persuasions argue, it is probably not to predetermined roles but to freedom, fullness, and, as Plato said, the exhilarating possibility of immortality. Sartre claimed that mankind is "condemned to freedom." With malice aforethought, he wrote that no one cares for us or about us. In Sartre's dark vision, ours is the loveless freedom of abandonment. We have been thoughtlessly dropped in a bleak region of a cheerless universe and doomed to a mortal freedom that leads inevitably to our death and personal dissolution.

But Christianity is a happier vision of our destiny: what appears at first to be the high melancholy of our fate is outreached by the higher hope of our faith. In God's providence our freedom is writ large and limitless and meant for our everlasting good.

† † †

## 22. Modern Disconnects

If Calvinism and similar movements portray man as a depraved creature selected for salvation by sovereign grace or condemned to perdition by divine rejection, the anthropological vision of the sciences that arose during the same era was even gloomier. Whereas in the Calvinistic anthropology man has fallen, in the scientific version he never rose to start with. According to Calvin only a few are saved from destruction; according to science, none.

This understanding of humanity denies from the start any transcendent destiny for mankind. As I stated earlier, it rested on the analytical assumption that whatever is lower and less complex is truer. Hence the modern assaults on human superiority and the mania to reduce the excellent to the ordinary, the advanced to the primitive, the intelligent to the instinctual, the animate to the inanimate.

At the same time the age of science was replete with counter movements and contradictions. Even though scientists of the first rank did not reject man's transcendent Christian faith but indeed shared it in most cases, the second-rate intellectuals of succeeding generations began an aggressive campaign against Christianity. Descartes, who epitomized the responsible intellectual climate of the seventeenth century and rightly has been called the father of modern philosophy, was not only a man of faith but a far more original thinker than Voltaire, the witty but irresponsible curmudgeon of the eighteenth-century *philosophes*. The pattern is as old as human history: the generations that inherit the creations of original minds tend to take their discoveries to extremes. Truth diminished is often truth exaggerated. In his writings we learn that Descartes had the courage of his Christian convictions, while by his actions we see that Voltaire had only the cowardice of his.

If medieval man could be proud of his soul modern man can only boast of his rights. The revolutionaries who fought to win our political rights in this world had little interest in our heavenly hopes in the next. Consequently, history has rendered its verdict: the harder they fought to set up heaven on earth, the more it resembled hell.

One may object that this was not the case of the American Revolutionaries. To which I would respond that there were no American Revolutionaries and nothing that could rightly be called an "American Revolution" as the term was understood in Europe. The Americans never intended to abolish the religion, customs, traditions, and institutions of their forefathers in the manner of the French Jacobins or the Russian Bolsheviks. If anything, the Americans of 1776 were more conservative than their British kinsmen and they desired their independence so they could freely and without abuse pursue their orderly and unpretentious Christian way of life.

On the other hand, in their zeal to establish the abstract rights of humanity the European zealots also sacrificed the freedoms—and often the lives—of real people. It is not generally understood that as the modern world has expanded our rights it has eroded our freedoms. Consider the lay of our lives: a daily despotism of laws, red lights, traffic signs, speed limits, prohibitions, codes, fines, deadlines, and penalties pressures our lives from birth to burial. In contrast think how free our ancestors were of such nuisances. In past centuries there were no traffic lights, no stop signs, no yellow lines—or white ones either—on their roads, no speed limits, licenses, or parking meters. And they could drive their uninspected and uninsured teams and carriages on either side of the undivided road they chose.

Not only this, but afoot and without penalty and usually without peril they, like the fabled chicken, could cross the road anywhere and any time they pleased. Consider also how free their children were from forced inoculations, compulsory testing, and obligatory school attendance. It is one of the arch paradoxes of our age that in the name of freedom much of life has become regulated and mandatory.

I say all this ironically, of course. We all know perfectly well that many of these restrictions and obligations are necessary in our congested world in which freedom and security are the promise but mandate and danger the reality. But aside from these comic aspects, it is sobering to remind ourselves at times that as we gain more abstract rights as a people, the fewer real freedoms we have as persons.

With the advent of Jacobin Revolution in 1789 and the effective demise of the old monarchies with their traditionally small and inept bureaucracies, the modern democratic State with its vastly increased power and efficiency replaced God as the author and guarantor of human rights. As far as individual freedom was concerned, the dictatorial monarchies of the few were replaced by the democratic tyranny of the many. But the philosophical flaw in this thinking was soon exposed as a political fallacy as well. For where the power of the State ends so do the rights it confers on its citizens, and when it falls so do the guarantees it offers.

In contrast, the Christian believes that his rights and freedoms are God-given and in Jeffersonian language, "unalienable." The primary duty of the State is to respect them above all else and defend them against violation and usurpation.

On a different note, many centuries ago, the medieval noblemen, like their barbaric Germanic ancestors, believed that a man's rights were connatural with his honor, manhood, and prowess and remained valid as far and as long as he could defend them. These were not rights as we understand them in the modern sense but personal privileges, literally one's personal laws (*privus* + *legis*=private law). A man was free as far as his skill, courage, and

HAROLD C. RALEY

strength could enforce them. It experienced a revival in frontier America and to this day has not entirely disappeared from the American psyche despite frequent conflicts with legal restrictions imposed by the modern democratic State, which prefers iconic figures who embody its imperfections to heroes who stand above them.

Modern people proclaim rights and freedom, but it is an open secret that security interests them even more. In *The Public Philosophy*, an old book (1955) that contains much wisdom, Walter Lippman points out that forced to make a choice between freedom and security, without hesitation most moderns would choose security. Erich Fromm and almost the whole existential school of his day went so far as to argue that freedom is a terrifying experience, particularly when it exposes one to loneliness, penury, hunger, and danger.

Distorted by ideologies of every stripe on the one hand and the reductionism of modern science on the other, modern anthropology as we are using the term here presents a dreary picture of contemporary mankind that leaves almost nothing to be admired and everything to be desired. We rush after gigantic pleasures but suffer gigantic boredoms. We build bigger houses but break up our homes. We demand truth but obey propaganda. We work to get ready to live tomorrow and life passes us by today. We plead for peace and fight those who disagree with us. We abhor racism yet color-code everybody. We stand for freedom provided it is mandated. We banish prayer and protect pornography. We tolerate everything but the intolerance of evil. We love humanity but despise our neighbors. We abort our children and adore our cats. We bomb foreign terrorists and subsidize our own. We demand stricter laws and law enforcement—for everybody else.

And so the ritual criticisms go in stylish intellectual circles. But after these fashionable flagellations the real question remains: what are our options? Which is the valid anthropology, which the true vision, the true hope of mankind?

Surely the one that always has been true: the Christian perspective of human life. For generations men and women in the Western World have experimented with alluring alternatives. After three hundred years of modern science, which tells us so much about the universe and so little about ourselves, we weary of learning about stars and galactic dust and hunger for nearer, dearer, livable truth.

To those who say we cannot return to a faith we have already tried and found wanting, I ask, when did we try it and how did it fail us? For as G. K. Chesterton responded in his day, those who reject Christianity do so without having lived the Christian life, for those who do discover its truth would not surrender it for the world.

In our day everything is a "world"—the sports world, woman's world, man's world, the animal world, the world of science, etc.—but a few realities really deserve the title. The West is one of them by virtue of its original Christian perspective. Here a caution rises before us. It is not easy—not to say impossible—to change the original orientation of such cultural "worlds." The Roman without Roman virtue, the Greek without Greek inquisitiveness, the Hebrew without reverence for God, the American without enterprise and faith do not simply become less than a former self but someone else altogether. There is always a historic penalty for abandoning the destiny that brought us this far. It begins with demoralization on a massive scale which commonly takes the form of immorality. We have lived so long in this state that we mistake moral illness for spiritual health.

All these considerations point us to the future, always the only way out of every plight and problem. Here sight yields to foresight. I said a couple of paragraphs ago that our best option for the future is the Christian perspective. But this is true only if there is truth left in Christianity. Is it, as its post-Christian critics assure us, a spent religion and a fool's fond dream that perished with our forefathers? Let us be truthful: everything else either has betrayed us or served us inadequately. Beginning with the Reformation, we of the West thought ourselves smarter than Christ and his Church and set out with high hopes of proving it. But it turns out centuries later that we were not wiser, and now we are haunted by the conviction that along the way of history we took a wrong turn. As our philosophies peter out in absurdities, our political dreams collapse into cynicism, and our makeshift churches drift into indifference we are thrown back on the only real hope we have left: the authentic Christian vision of human life.

Happily, it is more than enough. The world's worst has never been its match, nor for that matter, neither has its best.

# IV

# NEW THOUGHTS ON OLD THEMES

Sooner or later Christians curious to know the history and nature of their faith must confront the reality of the Middle Ages. Protestants generally dismiss the fifteen hundred years following the Apostolic Era as an age of suppression and error happily rectified at last by the Reformation. But this is a shocking, perhaps even heretical possibility; for it suggests that Christ himself was deluded when he promised that wickedness would not prevail against his Church. Was he wrong? Was the Church that he founded usurped and replaced for a millennium and a half by a counterfeit church? Or could it be that it is history and not Christ that stands in need of correction? These are some of the questions we shall consider in this chapter.

✝✝✝

## 23. Life and Belief in the Middle Ages

The age we moderns, or post-moderns if you prefer, consider to have been the epitome of faith, the much-reviled Dark Ages, was, comparatively speaking, less male-dominated than more enlightened Modern times. In the centuries before the modern predominance of ideas, sons and daughters of common families learned their respective traditional roles in close daily proximity. Nor did their lives and status greatly diverge with maturity and marriage but continued in the rude democratic equality that prevails when the sexes labor together in the urgent toils of livelihood.

But with the growth of universities and publishing an educational polarization occurred. Women—mothers, aunts, grandmothers, older sisters—continued in their customary role of teaching children the prevailing mores, manners, speech, stories, songs, games, dress, behavior, prohibitions, and religious practices. Girls, especially, learned the skills necessary for running their own homes. For many centuries this domestic instruction was—and to some degree still is—the primary meaning of "education" in several European languages. For many young men the story changed, as we shall soon see.

Almost none of this domestic education was formalized in writing but consisted rather of oral transmission. Reading and writing—rare skills in ages of belief—are generally associated with ideas and do not require personal contact. Learn to read and you read alone. On the other hand, oral tradition is closely linked to beliefs. "Faith comes from hearing," say the Scriptures, implying a close personal presence. The human loneliness and solitude of the modern centuries—an obsessive theme of poets and novelists—increased exponentially with the growth of literacy. The transmission of information and the telling of stories no longer required an immediate human presence. The literate world became an introverted world. The spoken word declined in importance and memory diminished. Illiterate people remember what they hear, for they must, just as they watch the speaker with greater intensity so as to discern the accuracy or falsity of the message. This probably helps explain the marked ability of many illiterate persons to discern honesty and deception in others. For their part, the literate often heed less what others say and how they say it, counting on and esteeming more highly the impersonal printed word. The stereotype of the absent-minded professor, that is, the supremely literate person who does not remember what others tell him, is surely an exaggeration, but an exaggeration of a truth.

It is interesting, but not surprising, to note that under the severe censorship of modern dictatorships the spoken word

90 *IV / New Thoughts on Old Themes*

recovers much of its lost prestige and often inspires a cycle of superior narrative literature. Because their very survival may depend on it, in times of great duress people learn anew to listen, to choose their words, and to remember what they hear. The word games that pass for philosophy in our day can flourish only in soft, pampered societies that have run short of true agendas. Serious times call for serious thought—and serious listening.

The diminished prestige of the spoken word in free societies, the nearly universal erosion of modern Western languages, and the corresponding decline of human memory have had a profound impact in many areas of modern life. In university teaching, for example, the classic lecture is today so ill esteemed and little remembered that many academicians now encourage alternate modes of imparting knowledge. The visual is steadily replacing the verbal. Rhetoric, once a cornerstone of medieval learning, has acquired an unsavory reputation and many people, perhaps approaching a majority, associate it with vacuous political oratory and take it to be a cynical exercise in duplicity. Parallels abound in many fields. In pastoral ministry sermons and homilies grow shorter and more colloquial; some bible translations have sunk to the level of common slang, and classic literature is beyond the capability—and certainly the interest—of many modern readers. The anti-philosophies of Deconstructionism and related doctrines (German thinker Martin Heidegger referred to similar movements in his day simply as *Destruktion*), which have as their basic premise the idea that language is either too defective to convey truth, if indeed it exists at all, or that at best it must be accepted on a fideistic level, as philosopher Ludwig Wittgenstein taught, are predictable consequences of this linguistic decline. But perhaps the cart has been put before the horse. Is it not the reader or the speaker who has first been deconstructed?

As the Middle Ages waned and vocations and opportunities expanded, many young men found it necessary to supplement domestic education described above with guild training and later with formal studies. Literacy ceased to be an exception and became a pragmatic expectation for those engaged in trades and professions. In the universities the growing intellectual class learned the intoxicating ideas of science, politics, and philosophy that were beginning to circulate. As their beliefs weakened, men replaced them with new theories and doctrines. Meanwhile, with rare exceptions women continued to live in the calmer realm of traditional beliefs.

For a long time stability and serenity were among woman's greatest charms. Seduced by glamorous intellectual creations, man found in belief-anchored woman a serene pace of life in which the enduring routine of daily activities contrasted with the frenzy of his ambition-driven existence. Precisely because she was grounded in immemorial beliefs woman often proved stronger and more resilient in the face of calamity and heartbreak. She could be counted on, and because she could, she was. If man was obsessed with theology, philosophy, poetry, politics, art, science, war, or commerce, woman was busy with the timeless chores of her home and the consolations of faith, family, and friends. In that era there was much validity in the observation that women maintain customs while men make laws. Valiant in his knowledge and voluble in his ideas, man often set out to master the world, and nearly as often he returned, careworn and wounded, to the charms and comforts offered by mysterious woman who took so little interest in his ideas and so much in him. It was no coincidence that the great age of lyricism arose when woman embodied a serener way of life and demonstrated a more elegant way of living it.

†✝†

## 24. The Renaissance

If it is true that modern Western mankind bears the indelible imprint of the medieval ethos, then to ponder its reality is to know more about ourselves. In an old but fascinating book *Love in the Western World*, Denis de Rougemont reasons that romantic love was convincingly the highest creation of that chivalric age. It opened up fabulously rich cycles of art and cultural refinement in Western civilization that have not yet entirely subsided. For even though Westerners think it a common feature of the human condition itself, courtly, romantic love has rarely, if ever, arisen natively in non-Western, non-Christianized lands.

Why not? We cannot say for certain, of course, but in its elevated, non-erotic sentiments and unselfish service to an ideal love, chivalry and courtly love suggest a secular parallel to the medieval Marian devotions. Can we not see in both the chivalrous knight and his lady transmutations of the Christian ideal of saints and saintly devotion to the Virgin? Can they be anything other than a Christian challenge to the pagan predominance of Eros?

If these suppositions are true, then we should not be surprised that as Christianity has waned in its homeland, primitive Eros has returned to reclaim his ancient pagan hegemony over human sentiment. Today love is again falling to the level of sexual eroticism while lyricism and romantic idealism are everywhere in retreat. The rich hoard of lofty sentiments deposited in the Christian psyche is nearly spent. Like a divine but dying flame rarely does the courtly idealism flare today with noble reminders of higher loves.

The decline of the chivalric and romantic ideal is more injurious than we know. Over many generations the Western psyche was configured to these ideals of faith, love, and high devotion and nothing else would suffice to fill the void. Today we are stuffed with alternatives to romantic love and parodies of courtly devotion, yet despite our surfeit of substitutes we hunger still and all the more for genuine spiritual nourishment. It is a hunger peculiar to Christianized, or once Christianized peoples, for it is rooted in a long history that other peoples do not fully share and therefore do not understand or suffer to the same degree as

Christians or former Christians. This does not mean that outsiders cannot understand this peculiarity of the Western ethos. Indeed, it would be enlightening to Westerners to see themselves explained by non-Westerners of good will. I insist on the good will, for insights arising out of the plentiful and prevailing ill will of our time serve no useful human purpose I know of.

What was the "Renaissance"? Johan Huizenga wrote that Erasmus understood the term in its original Christian meaning of "rebirth." But if we interpret it in the common way to mean a break with the medieval past, then I can only conclude with C. S. Lewis that *there was no Renaissance*, just as I argue that there were no "Dark Ages." Our historiographical terminology describes our history neither accurately nor honorably. What we call the Renaissance was not a "rebirth," as the term literally implies, but the magnificent maturity of artistic, philosophic, political trends and ideals that had been budding and growing in European civilization for a thousand years. It was not the end of the medieval past with its chivalric and Christian ideals but its maturity and fruition.

In art the medieval Christian motifs were not abandoned in the so-called "Renaissance" but brought to unsurpassed perfection. From the earliest Roman/Byzantine-inspired works, through the Romanesque to the Gothic, and finally in the sublime art of the "Renaissance" we can trace the successive artistic and architectural stages in the slow but steady development of the Christian ideal.

Are we, like the Modern Age, to scorn so quickly the age that built the Romanesque and Gothic cathedrals of Europe, inspired the world's greatest artistic tradition, and produced the likes of St. Anselm, St. Thomas Aquinas, St. Catherine, and St. Francis of Assisi? We do only if we have fallen so low as to deserve scorn ourselves, for all these achievements belong to the spiritual heritage of Western civilization. The truths we mock have a way of coming back to mock us. The civilization that shaped the Christian and chivalric ideals and inspired centuries of the world's most refined piety, art, theology, and learning deserves not our contempt but our admiration, more, our gratitude. Our modern literature, for example, is rooted in the cycle of Arthurian legends; our modern thought—and ultimately our science—rests on a medieval foundation of theology and philosophy; our modern languages are a medieval legacy, and for that matter so is medieval Latin, which surely would have died with the Roman Empire but for generations of monks and medieval scholars; and our very Christianity—Catholic and Protestant—would be an unrecognizable sect without a thousand years of medieval piety and enlightened theology. We stand on the shoulders of anonymous giants who were too modest to seek our forms of modern personal notoriety. The modern mania for originality which we discussed earlier was almost unknown amongst medieval people. Take away the Middle Ages and we would be reduced to cultural beggary and spiritual impoverishment. Take away its Christian foundation and lyricism soon wilts like an unwatered flower.

In his hostility to medieval theology, Martin Luther thought he had vanquished St. Thomas Aquinas and Aristotle with a superior understanding (dramatized in Hans Holbein the Younger's superb woodcut *The German Hercules*). With similar antipathies the Enlightenment thinkers and Napoleon announced that they would abolish Christianity itself. In each case, they boasted prematurely. And now we begin to understand why. From our longer historical perspective it becomes clearer that regardless of personal genius no single individual can supplant the collective religious wisdom of an entire historical age. Second, despite its shortcomings, the Middle Ages was much more rooted in truth than the Modern Age dreamed.

Protestant Christianity deserves praise for revitalizing its ancient Apostolic heritage. But often it ignored its medieval past, dismissing it as centuries of Catholic error. Surely one of the great imperatives of our time, our so-called "post-Modern" era, will be to resurrect the medieval heritage of all Christians and bring it to plenitude. It will not be a return to the past but the rediscovery of its treasury of truths on which to build a more humanized world, which we take to mean a more Christianized future.

† † †

## 25. On Tolerance

From a different angle let us turn again to the theme of tolerance. It is one of the shibboleths of modern intellectual and religious discourse. Indeed we would not be far wrong to say that we live under the tyranny of tolerance. Not surprisingly, as Christianity declines in its old heartland it yields to this general mandate and appears to grow more tolerant and prone to compromise. Yet we need to remind ourselves that Christian tolerance had an inglorious beginning. It first arose as a result of the stalemate in the religious wars of the sixteenth and seventeenth centuries and was neither a consequence of military victory nor an act of Christian generosity but an acknowledgment of weariness and the inability of either side to win the struggle. Only modern Western ethics has attempted to convert it to virtue.

The early Christians were replete with virtues, but tolerance of evil was not among them. Hence their martyrdom. This is why in cultures where the modern Western ethos has not penetrated notions of religious tolerance are weak. Much of the world looks with cynical incredulity on the "tolerant" Western notion that every conflict has at least two valid sides and can be mediated by compromise to the partial defeat of both. For non-Westerners this odd inclination to willful defeat appears to be not only an act of incomprehensible stupidity but a contradiction of truth and therefore must conceal either a weakness or a cynical deception, or more likely, both. Hence the mediocre record of Western diplomacy based on the modern model of tolerance.

The struggles of the Reformation shook the foundations of Christianity, causing what had been its age-old, unquestioned beliefs to break from their moorings, to rise to the surface, to become visible, and, in sum, to cease to be unconscious beliefs and take on the polemical characteristics of ideas. As ideas they were now subject to debate, to passion, to hatred, to obsolescence. Suddenly men came forth armed with new interpretations of history and Scripture to defend, reform, or reject what Western Christians had taken for granted for fifteen centuries.

But their zeal to defend and attack opposing versions of the Christian faith jeopardized the core Christian beliefs, the "mere Christianity" described by C.S. Lewis. For when people defend beliefs they expose them and convert them into conscious ideas, which one then may take or leave. And what we can take or leave, we always leave eventually. In the long run, the ideological victor stands to lose as much as the loser. For win or lose, beliefs that have weakened to ideas seldom recover their former predominance. In the case of Christianity, what had been the unquestioned human condition for centuries now became a matter of choice not of faith alone but also of the militant ideas that now sprang up and surrounded Christianity.

In these polemical circumstances an adversarial co-dependency soon developed between Catholic and Protestant Christians. By their very name the latter point to an original parasitical relationship to Catholicism. The empty Protestant cross, for instance, makes sense only if we refer it historically to the Catholic crucifix. And in a protest once removed, this time against the Protestants themselves, the unadorned plainness of a Quaker church without cross, or crucifix, or art of any sort, can be understood only if we recall the ornate iconography of the early Church and the successive iconoclastic purges of later times.

The dissenters could be Protestants only by protesting against something. This is obvious and has been pointed out many times before. What is not so apparent is that Catholicism also took on certain Protestant-like attributes.

For just as Protestants depended adversarially on Catholicism, so Catholicism ceased to speak unchallenged for all Christendom, or at least Western Christendom, and commenced to substantiate its claims to Apostolic legitimacy by polemic comparisons to what it considered to be new apostate varieties of Christianity. In short, by protesting against Protestantism, Catholicism itself also became somewhat Protestant.

† ✝ †

## 26. Women in the Age of Imperialism

The Chinese yin/yang rhythm of human life and history seems both attractively appealing and overly simplistic from a Western perspective. Still it would be hard to deny it a certain validity since with observable periodicity, which interestingly enough appears to coincide roughly with the centuries, some eras appear to be dominated by masculine characteristics, just as others incline to the feminine. This motion is not like the swings of a pendulum, however, but may be more accurately, though not completely, described as a spiral. History is not fatalistic repetition; things never simply repeat themselves nor return to their former place, even though there is a similarity of tendencies.

Nor must we suppose that women necessarily predominate in these feminine eras or centuries, or that they are totally submerged in the times of masculine ascendancy. It is not a question of sexuate superiority but alternating dynamics of life that affect men and women with equal force but in different ways. There is a further caution: we are not dealing with arithmetically exact delineations, which apply only to abstract beings and schemata, but with human reality, which permits only approximations. In its rightful place precision is a virtue, often a small one, but it can become an error when forcibly imposed on human reality. With this in mind, let us consider some examples.

The eighteenth century is the best near historical example of a feminine century. Precious in the French sense [*précieux*] and not coincidentally concentrated in France, it was a wonderfully verbal, verbose, and visual age when everything worth saying was said in the most graceful way possible, a time of exquisite manners, scintillating conversation, wit, games, gaiety, repartee, parties, fashion, food, gossip, and elevated, if not always decent, taste. Sexuality was relaxed, and what we might call immorality was acceptable, even expected, but nothing gross, heavy, or vulgar in art, literature, or behavior was permitted. Rococo art, which avoided the massive and tended to the miniature and the delicate, replaced the heavier Baroque of the seventeenth century. The nineteenth-century music of Wagner likely would have horrified sensitive Enlightenment audiences whose ears were attuned to the likes of Bach and Vivaldi. Not surprisingly, French audiences of Voltaire's time (who translated portions of Shakespeare's plays) found the English dramatist to be too extravagant and barbaric for their tastes. On the other hand, the French *philosophes* lavished praise on the English for their balance and restraint in government. Above all, it was a hospitable age and as its embodiment France welcomed civilized people from every country. Writing over a century later, French dramatist Henri de Bournier repeated a deeply held conviction of earlier times: "Every man has two countries, his own and then France."

Without necessarily being effeminate, the best masculine minds of the eighteenth century exhibited the qualities listed earlier that we normally associate more with the feminine. Not surprisingly, it was also a century of extraordinary women who just as they directed the affairs of society and the arts with their intellect and strength of character so they directed the king and kingdom with their amorous affairs. And as France went in the eighteenth century so the rest of Western civilization aspired to go. All civilized countries measured themselves by French standards.

In sharp contrast, the nineteenth century began under a masculine sign. The *Ancien Régime* and all its glamour was swept away by the Revolution and its busy guillotine. Remembering the glories of the genteel eighteenth century, Tallyrand remarked that no one who had not lived in the Paris of 1780 could possibly know how good life could be.

As paradoxical as it may seem, the rise of political parties in the new regimes of the nineteenth century, at once a consequence and a means of spreading revolutionary democracy in the West, diminished the standing and influence of women. For well over a century the radical democratic doctrine that all men were created equal did not extend to women, nor of course did it include all men. Palace politics at which women excelled in the pre-revolutionary *Ancien Régime* gave way to popular plebiscites from which women were excluded until well into the twentieth century.

The predominance of male attitudes is unmistakable in the nineteenth century. It was the grand epoch of territorial aggression and empire building, and not only in geopolitics but also in science, philosophy, literature, and music. The lords of each discipline—Napoleon, Darwin, Freud, Marx, Nietzsche, Hegel, Dickens, Balzac, Wagner, Rhodes, the American imperialists, etc.—each with a transcendent vision, tried to make the world his fiefdom and each took it upon himself to speak and act universally—*urbi et orbi*—for all humanity under his purview. It would be impossible for us to understand the cynicism and jaded minimalism of our time without first being aware of the extraordinary ambitions and exuberant optimism of the nineteenth century. Its sweeping panorama was a supremely masculine vision with only a nod to the distaff side of humanity. Better said perhaps, the gifted women of that time also lived and worked under the aegis of the masculine and barely resembled in their attitudes the ladies who set the tone and monitored the tastes of the eighteenth century.

The nineteenth century accelerated a process begun much earlier. Since the Enlightenment, and to some degree even earlier, the area of beliefs, the traditional spiritual abode of average women, has been shrinking, and along with it her prestige and importance. Today the standing of woman—as woman—has seldom been lower. I refer not to her abstract legal rights based on democratic ideals of equality to which she has full claim, but to actual, belief-anchored prerogatives that in an earlier time woman exercised freely in her home and private relationships.

The erosion of beliefs has left woman with a smaller "territory" in which to shape her once traditional life. She has been forced out of her private space and into the public male-dominated arena. Like man centuries earlier, she has exchanged her old beliefs for an idea-driven life. Probably this is why contemporary woman often gives the impression of naively, at times awkwardly, committing the same errors and repeating the same vices that man mastered—or more precisely mastered him—long ago. She copied rather than corrected the mistakes of men.

As she abandoned her belief-centered life and veered in step with idea-driven man, woman lost much of her traditional enchantment. As she ventured to work elbow to elbow with man, familiarity robbed her of mystery. Regardless of her personal beauty, with the loss of distance she declined in grace and elegance, always the essence of femininity. Because of this decline, she ceased to be man's lyric inspiration and became his friend, partner, or rival, a female version of everyman and handyman. She was less inclined and less able to comfort man in his woes and as likely to recite her own unlovely list of miseries. And as her charm declined so did lyricism, so did poetry, so did what we once called "romance."

And so did marriage. Contemporary Western woman satisfies fewer desires and therefore corresponds to fewer needs in man and family. For example, the State has taken over the education of children—both in the primary and secondary meanings we saw earlier—and medical professionals see to their health. Clothing is abundant and relatively inexpensive, which means that she is no longer required to be an expert seamstress. Furthermore, modern birth controls and legal abortion mean that for the first time in the history of womanhood sexuality and childbearing have been biologically separated. Consequently, in recent decades sexual activity has lost much of its familial and moral sanctity, along with its traditional allegiance to love and alliance with marriage, and has come to be seen as merely another pleasure, if not a right, available in or out of wedlock. Seemingly shorn of its old consequences and commitments, sex has sunk from the transcendent to the trivial in a wrenching social upheaval that could be described as the general promiscuity of our time. There is no need to rehearse here the mournful litany of loneliness, sorrow, disease, and human wreckage brought on by this new "liberation" except to suggest that in the name of freedom both sexes are busily forging heavier chains for themselves.

The domestic love and attention woman once lavished as a prerogative of her condition as wife, mother, and grandmother, she often views today as an imposition on her time and an infringement on her profession. Families drift apart and marriages dissolve. The trend has widened to universal dimensions. The Western world has wrenched free from its ancient moorings and may be swirling towards some mysterious future configuration. And as it does so it destabilizes much of the rest of the world. We are beggared for permanence in life's cardinal points. The contemporary is temporary. What we see about us is like a movie set: real in appearance but liable to be dismantled and replaced at any moment.

For these reasons we must not conclude that the apparent masculinization of life in modern times has increased man's happiness at woman's expense. Nor should we forget that even though the imperial dreams of modern Western mankind began with great optimism, they ended poorly. The forms of decline suggested here, along with others not mentioned, represent absolute losses, that is, human losses that diminish both sexes. There is an inviolable rule in

THE LIGHT OF EDEN

human life that when woman is unhappy, man is miserable. When woman loses her calming serenity man's characteristic restlessness increases exponentially. Without the steadying hand of woman to make his house a home man drifts aimlessly, but nearly always in the direction of things evil, almost never towards things good.

It is an irony of history that men birthed Christianity and women nourished it. From the first female witnesses to the Resurrection, extraordinary numbers of women were drawn to the Christian faith. Nor did this attraction cease over the ages. Throughout the centuries, men who "never darkened church door" were pleased to have their wives, daughters, mothers, sisters, and other female relatives "represent" them and hold the door open for their own sporadic attendance. Though impossible to prove, it is yet not unreasonable to say that in nearly every era the intensity of faith was much greater in women than in men. Men were willing to fight for Christianity, to defend it in battles and crusades, to give their lives to preserve it. But they were less likely to live their faith through daily prayer and devotion. It was the steady faith of women that proved to be the strongest pillar of Christianity.

Now this pillar is weakening, another casualty of the drastic changes that transformed masculine life in earlier times and now shifts to feminine life with similar results in recent decades. The impoverishment of belief and the uncontrolled proliferation of ideas, now common to both sexes, put Christianity at risk.

# V

## THE SACRED AND THE SECULAR

Will Christianity die of broadmindedness? G. K. Chesterton asked the question in his day, and it bears repeating in ours. We know the pattern: what begins as a courageous acceptance of the unbiblical ends up a cowardly surrender to the unchristian. For the more Christianity tolerates wrong the more wrongs it must tolerate. Once advantaged, evil sheds the false meekness that won it sympathy and puts good to rout, for it honors no pact, returns no favor, shows no gratitude, and respects no boundary. Its ambitions are limitless and its aim is always to unleash the next obscenity in society.

† † †

### 27. Society and Second Thoughts

What is society and how is it structured? For the sake of later clarity on several points let us give a partial answer to this double question. According to popular sociology, the family is society's model and basic building block. Jean-Jacques Rousseau, who conceived the idea in the eighteenth century, argued that society is not only made up of family units but also resembles an extended family in its total structure. But if we think about it, we see that this neat architectural image simply is not so. If it were, the high percentages of divorce and family collapse would quickly and fatally weaken and destroy society, as proponents of the family theory predict almost daily. Yet plainly this is not what happens. The breakup of marriages and families is a tragic phenomenon fraught with grave moral, human, and economic implications for the social collectivity, but the social powers themselves continue in force regardless of what happens to individuals and families.

Society, we discover, is not an edifice built of structural units and pieces but first of all a dynamic balance of impersonal or transpersonal forces consisting of binding beliefs, customs, behaviors, laws, protocols, prohibitions, punishments, usages, expectations, conventions, assumptions, traditions, mores, and silent suppositions in play within a human collectivity. We could think of these forces as vectors pushing in several, even opposing directions, but which taken together produce an ever-shifting equilibrium. At any given moment some are intensifying, others have peaked, and still others are declining.

It is important for our understanding to make a distinction between the masses of people and society. Naturally they are inseparable, but inseparably distinct. If by some magical power we could remove groups of individuals from their several societies and deposit them all together in an unpopulated area, we would have a mass of persons but not a society.

Rousseau argued that society consists of an unspoken daily plebiscite, a free association of people in what he called a "social contract." He went on to claim that mankind has the inherent right at any given time to abrogate the contract in case, say, of abuse or tyranny, for human freedom is inalienable. Despite his oversimplification of social reality—or perhaps because of it—Rousseau's reasoning became the intellectual underpinning for a series of modern revolutions and to this day remains one of the questionable principles—a belief—of Western democracy. His writings are a combination of seductive insights and chilling oversights, which despite his defective reasoning has had a seminal influence in shaping modern education, sociology, and political theory.

Generally speaking, societies coincide with the political

and linguistic boundaries of nations, but they are more fluid than artificial borders and may extend fully or partially over several countries. What we call the "Western World" is an example of a partial society, but the subject is too vast for this context. For our purposes at the moment, it is enough to remember that society is an enforced collective worldview within which is interlaced comfortably or incompatibly our personal belief structure introduced in the previous section.

Individually we may choose to disobey certain social mandates, but the inconveniences and punishments that flow from antisocial behavior reveal in an obverse way the force society exerts on us. Furthermore, in normal situations one must belong to a society in order to disobey its social rules. For social rebellion is also an expression of social belonging, a form of what sociologist Gabriel Tarde called "counter imitation." Were I in China, for example, I might unintentionally offend Chinese sensitivities by my foreign behavior, but within my own society it cannot be said that I violate Chinese social norms because they are not in force in my circumstances. The Bible states that "the stranger" is to be treated with respect—and wary circumspection—but as a Gentile he is obliged only to respect the Judaic laws, not to conform to them. The phenomenon of social groups encysted in encircling societies is delicate in any era and susceptible to explosive tensions in ours, as the controversial writings of Edward Said forcefully illustrate.

In theory, at any given moment everyone could individually dissent from social norms, just as everybody could be divorced and every family dissolved, yet the binding social forces themselves, like the unseen atmosphere, would continue to exert their impersonal pressure on us. Law, for instance, as a subset of the broader social forces does not depend on our compliance in order to exercise its power. Countless people may protest a law, may violate it, but that does not lessen initially its binding force or change the consequences of the violation.

This does not mean that society consists wholly or even primarily of punitive powers. Ideally, society itself exists to make individual life as safe and free as possible. Its impersonal norms resolve many of our problems and make life easier for us. Without conventional protocols of conduct, for instance, our first encounters with strangers could be fearful challenges. We would not know whether to greet them, run from them, or attack them. Lacking socially sanctioned patterns of courtesy, we would spend our life wrestling with these everyday trivialities. (This, by the way, is what happens in viciously deteriorated societies. Every person is a possible menace and every encounter a potential threat to wellbeing.) Society furnishes us prior solutions to these common situations. By means of prevailing social protocol we have a reasonable idea of how others will act towards us and, in turn, how we are to behave towards them. This done, we are free to move on to more important matters.

Some consider social niceties to be hypocrisy and choose to ignore them. But they miss the point and overlook the excellent purpose these modest protocols serve. Good manners make good sense. The Bible teaches the sanctity and shows the rewards of hospitality. Consider Abraham's gracious behavior towards the three angels who appeared before his camp on the plains of Mamre to announce the eventual birth of Isaac and to prepare the destruction of Sodom and Gomorrah. Imagine what might have been his fate, including the fate of his covenant with God, had he been discourteous to these powerful beings.

Like beliefs, social norms originate as admirable individual behaviors and ideas that people imitate in ever widening circles until they reach the level and acquire the power of prevailing social assumptions. In the beginning every human invention is an individual creation, or more likely, a novel recombination of preexisting knowledge. Despite our mystical reverence for the masses in this democratic age, there is no mass invention or art. We may attribute creativity to the masses because we cannot identify the individual originators. But this is a consequence of ignorance and not an accurate attribution. As Ortega wrote in *The Revolt of the Masses*, in their normal role the masses do not invent but more or less docilely adopt and imitate admired behaviors. Every successful salesman knows how to manipulate the normal susceptibility of individuals to suggestion and instruction. Despite their protestations of independence, normally people do as they are told, especially in moments of uncertainty. It is the principle of propaganda, not surprisingly the same word used for advertising in some languages.

Yet social forces have their limits, and over time persistent violations can erode their power. After years of continuous assaults many social forces have weakened, and elementary uncertainty over antisocial behaviors is reemerging to consume more of our time. "Break the rules" has itself become a counter rule and to those who dutifully obey it, a selling slogan for everything from cigarettes to sports cars. Naturally this strategy presupposes that there are still rules to break. What happens when the last rules are broken for good is anybody's guess but everybody's problem.

Contrary to what Rousseau believed, the family is essentially the opposite of society, and the threshold of the home forms the boundary between the two spheres. The family is our refuge from society, as society can be our escape from the family. Family breakups do tragic harm to people, but the damage they wreak on the social structure is negligible. Of course the family also exists in society and is subject at several levels to its forces. Yet it does not create those powers but preserves an intimate character that by definition society cannot possess.

✝✝✝

## 28. Society and Secularized Religion

American society includes at a basic level the forceful belief that the tolerance discussed in the previous section has priority over contending religious and political doctrines. Exaggerating to make the point, we could say it is the secular religion of social tolerance. As an immediate benefit in the religious arena this broadmindedness allows a bewildering assortment of churches and creeds to coexist in civil peace. But this social gain is offset by a certain invalidation of the respective church doctrines themselves. Because all, or nearly all, dogmas have a right to admission under the big tent of social tolerance, by a slight shift in that same right they can claim to be equally worthy as dogma. Social tolerance usually translates into religious respectability. Yet even though socially accepted and tolerant in their external application, internally these dogmas may be harshly incompatible with other creeds. But no matter; few believers—and proportionately few preachers, pastors, and priests—enforce these teachings in all their intended seriousness anyway. To a certain degree nearly every church in America has become a heresy of itself.

Having assimilated this broad social tolerance, great numbers of Christians have little attachment to any creed and as often as not treat the historical denominational articles of their faith with surprising indifference. Antiquity, which itself once was invested with authority and inspired respect, has become in our day a general disqualifier; the older a thing is the less we feel inclined to take it seriously.

In passing, we can say the same about people. The modern centuries reversed the immemorial roles of youth and age. In former times people believed the limited happiness possible in this world was to be found in the wisdom of the elderly, but in recent times they are more likely to associate it with the foolishness of the young. Hence the pathetic attempts to prolong youth beyond its time and the saccharine euphemisms that disguise age.

Lacking creedal loyalty, many Christians have become religious nomads, wandering in doctrinal detachment from church to church and even from religion to religion, convinced that there are many roads to salvation, none strait, all broad, and tolerantly persuaded that God would not condemn as wrong what society holds as right. Under these conditions the discipline once proper to liturgical churches becomes next to impossible. The sheep have taken to herding the shepherd, and, more, will desert the pastor's flock at the slightest provocation and scurry indignantly to another.

I have outlined these general features of religious tolerance without including the hypocrisy that often accompanies it. Briefly put, in the interest of civil harmony, society requires that we turn a blind eye and give a smile to many unacceptable things. One paradoxical result is that even though we have the legal right of free speech, we lack the social right to speak freely. In many sectors of modern life the social injunction either to keep silent or to speak hypocritically of the very things we may earnestly detest has become operatively stronger than the legal right to exercise free speech. As a result, the greater the offenses committed against social harmony, the more the pressures build in our day to say nothing offensive against them. The rougher the waves, the less we talk about the rocking boat. Indeed the blame for the offense often shifts to those who do dare to speak out and the offenders themselves are sympathetically honored as victims.

But if seldom deceived, we are often betrayed by this social hypocrisy. We dismiss public utterances as so many lies that must be translated into truth. The danger is that it is but a short step from this attitude to cynicism, which is the unwillingness, finally the inability, to recognize truth at all. For the cynic the only truth is the absence of truth. He takes pride in never being deceived—and for this very reason always is.

Because of these social falsehoods never was more said publicly but less believed privately. Unless trends change, within a few years this social pressure against uncensored speech likely will take the form of legal prohibitions as well, probably under the rubric of so-called "hate legislation." For what people do—perhaps hypocritically at first—in time they come to accept as normal; and what they accept as normal they convert to belief, and what they believe builds into the binding social force described earlier.

✝✝✝

## 29. A Prediction

Human things are not inevitable. If they were, there would be no human history, and for that matter no human intelligence as we know it. For above all, history is the story of choices made and chances uniquely won and lost. And history in the making flows from the same existential challenge we face every day: in order to go on living we must go on doing something. But exactly what we must do, the content and intent of our daily doing, is our decision to make. Our possibilities are always plural, and this is why history is never the same history. We can always change our mind as long as we have a mind to change. We are invested with an ineradicable freedom.

For this reason, but for the incalculable human grief they have caused, we could dismiss as ridiculous all theories of historical inevitability of the sort that Karl Marx preached. After all, Marx himself was the first to violate his supposedly inviolable principles of economic determinism. The very fact that we can decide to argue for deterministic inevitability is the best proof against it. For we cannot argue for determinism without considering its alternatives, else there could be no argument in the first place. If our life were really predetermined we would not be aware of it and could not think about it at all, much less try to prove it. A stone thrown in the air does not question the physical laws that determine where it will fall. People, on the other hand, debate everything under the sun, including their supposed lack of freedom and free will, precisely because they have freedom and free will. Would-be determinists squabble and thus disprove their premise, for determinism does not permit debate.

Because of life's plural possibilities, all predictions, no matter how well grounded in probabilities, are liable to error. And in our age the fear of error has grown greater than our devotion to truth. But this attitude is itself a

THE LIGHT OF EDEN

mistake: to be intimidated by the chance of error is to have committed the first one already.

Prediction is further complicated by the radical contingency of the unforeseen. In 1492 Europeans—and Native Americans—were established within their respective worlds. For all their circumstantial discomforts, they were set in their ways and settled in their condition, and nothing on the horizon seemed likely to change their way of life. Yet what really happened was as unforeseeable as the white sails of Columbus' ships rising one October day on the horizon of the blue Caribbean Sea. And so it is with human events: from out of nowhere, at least nowhere we expect, chance or a higher power intervenes from time to time to break up our settled schemes, disrupt our old patterns, and restore us again to creative freedom. At certain crucial moments of history humanity is privileged to recreate the world.

Mindful of these precautionary comments and contingencies, I make the following prediction, not as an inevitability which I have already argued against, but as a probability that can occur unless things change, unless there is a general veering away from present trends—always a possibility. Everywhere there are symptoms that democracy is beginning to turn malignant and proving to be no exception to the rule that all forms of human governance eventually fail and that in draconian upheavals mankind shall have to begin anew.

The notion persists that democracy is the delicious fruit of intellectual enlightenment and the economic means of production. But history tells us otherwise. It was not the means of production that gave birth to democracy in Greece but rather the means of destruction. Until the Persian Wars only free-born noblemen waged war in Athens and other Greek cities. But threatened by massive invasions from the East, the Athenians and their neighbors had no choice but to mobilize much larger armies and navies. And the obligation to bear arms, first for defense and later for imperialistic expansion, led automatically to political engagement by the

V / The Sacred and the Secular   113

disenfranchised classes. The same phenomenon occurred in Rome and again in nineteenth-century Europe. Throughout the European Middle Ages war was a privilege that European noblemen jealously guarded as their birthright. Only when peasants were needed for massive imperialistic armies did they begin to acquire political influence. Throughout history democracy and militaristic imperialism have gone hand in hand. The American slogan of World War II, "old enough to fight, old enough to vote," was only the latest example of how military service spreads democracy. It does not come from the barrel of a rifle, as radical revolutionaries would have us believe, but from the other end, from the one who holds and aims the rifle.

In a later chapter I shall take up the question of Machiavellianism, that is, the deliberate, planned manipulation of evil, and its pernicious effects on modern life. Here I need only note that democratic governments have embraced this ethical perversion with practically the same enthusiasm as the despots.

What nations proclaim as their proudest virtue often turns out to be also their profoundest vice. So it is with the modern Western infatuation with democratic governance. Democracy probably is, as Winston Churchill once said in so many words, the best of imperfect political systems. But a system that reduces its citizens to a cipher and decides their most urgent matters by a plurality of numbers possesses no absolute superiority that I can see over other systems. Furthermore, when citizens discover that by their mere numbers they can gain access to the public treasury and vote themselves largesse they place democracy under the perennial threat of fiscal bankruptcy.

Naturally, democracy can be a magnificent system of governance—but only with a magnificent populace. Democracy governs well only when people first govern themselves with the self-reliance that Ralph Waldo Emerson preached. And much the same may be said of other forms of governance, at least it can be said of those that place the wellbeing of its citizens above ideology. Given this primal condition, all systems rise and fall on the ethical strength and self-discipline of its people. The votes of a vicious populace will be as ruinous to human welfare as the whims of a vicious tyrant. And the first leads inevitably to the second, for those who abuse freedom will soon lose it to tyranny. A noble people will create a noble government in its likeness, and a debased people will establish a corrupt government in its image. In general and with exceptions, people get the government they deserve.

Modern democracy replaced princes with plebiscites and set up a system of divided powers whereby people determined to rule without a ruler. But the specter of the banished sovereign seems to prowl about in the psyche of Western mankind, and the checks and balances of our democracies are strategies to prevent the return of the king. Every successful politician is a potential threat to democracy. Democracy succeeds when politicians fail.

The immoral debris accumulating about us is the characteristic litter that gathers in the wake of sinking human systems. In their youthful beginnings nearly all forms of governance show their primal vigor and virtue; in their decline, they reveal their genetic flaws. Age magnifies the inherent defects of all organisms. Young democracies rise on the virtues of its people, but in their waning stages they expand law to fill the vacuum left by a dying ethics. But to no lasting avail, for in the end democratic republics perish as much from a surfeit of law as from an excess of lawlessness. They are the two sides of the same coin.

In our day breakdowns are occurring on all sides. Our best efforts and greatest expenditures are no longer creative but curative. Our age has turned remedial, which indicates that we may be entering the final phases of our democracy. It is late to save our democratic world, but not yet too late. Unlike W. B. Yeats' grim poetic vision of the future, the center still holds but decay is spreading at the margins.

✝✝✝

## 30. Huge and Hurried

We live in an age of the colossal, which often is a harbinger of impending collapse. When the genetic and social barriers to excessive growth weaken, cities sprawl even as they rot from within, republics swell into empires before dying, governments bloat into bureaucracies, and animal species grow huge before extinction. Today this feature lies close to our heart. Obsessed with gigantism in all its forms, we push for records and think we have accomplished nothing unless we do it more and faster than our predecessors and competitors. For in all things we are comparative. Thinking it freedom, we yearn for infinite space and bear a cordial hatred towards limits. Roads that end frustrate and sadden us, and at land's end we would rush on to far free worlds beyond the sea. Yet we are pressed by human proximity: the mere congestion of the world slows our mighty races to a crawl.

The past now seems too little to bind us in loyalty to its truths. From our modern vastness we look back on the world of our forefathers and see only dwarfish quaintness. For we think we have outgrown its limits and moralities. Old virtues hard won in yesterday's toils are soon squandered in today's indulgences. We are less than ourselves yet consider inferior all who lived before or will live after us. As George Orwell said, "every generation imagines itself to be more intelligent than the one that went before it, and wiser than the one that comes after it."

Let us not be duped by dimensions on a map. The colossal is not just a matter of size. There are, for example, geographically greater lands than America, yet none conceived on so vast a proportional scale. The broad expanses of many countries are seen as uninviting wastelands or dreary peasant provinces at the fringes of a concentrated, unshared civilization. As their supreme punishment in former times, disgraced Chinese officials were banished to the far western deserts of Sinkiang, while Russians were exiled to the Siberian East for similar offenses. In both cases, these distant lands belonged to their countries, but their countries did not belong to them. Historically China and Russia shielded themselves with their frontier territories, and as a military strategy, they were always ready to sacrifice the provinces to save the relatively small capital core.

On the other hand, the frontier lands similar to those the Chinese and Russians used for military defense and political exile the Americans seized as opportunity. The Americans went west not in exile but in expectation, and American civilization went with them. For them these distant lands were not beyond the pale but a happy expansion of the pale. America never thought of itself as a precious, elitist center surrounded and shielded by vast outer territories. Instead it quickly expanded to occupy its entire continental extent. California was soon as fully American as Virginia or Massachusetts and as readily protected. There were no sacrificial territories and no all-absorbing capital, which is still the rule in much of the world. Instead, America has many centers and many alternatives, and if one declines in style and vigor another arises to replace it. In this sense, America is incomparably the largest of the nations. Yet as large as it is, in relation to its normal vastness America can also become morbidly colossal. Every country seems to be genetically programmed to reach a certain size normal for it, and additional growth triggers degeneration.

Speed is the correlate of the colossal and shares its pathology. There is a malign force in the world rushing us to our destination so that we will miss our destiny. Born at the end of a slower era, I cannot stifle an old yearning to stop and walk in intimate converse with the roads that pass by in dizzying haste and hills where I can sit and soak in views that perhaps none other admires. Certified vistas bludgeon us with their lush official beauty, but the truer test of our aesthetics is to coax forth the imperfect enchantments of lands that never poet praised or artist painted. Traveling alone—for others are impatient—in atonement for my usual haste, I stop to stroll down a pathway, to touch a rock and ponder its secrets, to get my feet on the ground and renew my old romance with the world and childish apprehension of snakes and spiders. Nothing is more pleasurable than to return to the child locked within us and dare to play again. We do so when no one looks, of course, for the force that urges us mocks the cosmic delight we call child's play. Perhaps no one has ever touched this pebble or explored that stream before, never sensed their eagerness to bare their small immemorial charms. Each new discovery reveals a secret to us about ourselves, and each adds a modest virtue to our understanding. We ascend in solitary renewals. Amid the passing trees I single one out and hold it in fleeting friendship, imagining its seasons of sapling youth and mature grandeur and striving to find its kinship with my life. Have I seen it before? Will I ever see it again? Then it is gone, and each farewell is a reminder of mortality. The ideal, were there world enough and time, would be to consider each thing fully in its place, to acknowledge it as the center of creation—for it is—and with loving solicitude celebrate its connections to its unheralded neighbors, its infinite links to realities that stretch out of sight, and its final dimensions we know as God. There is an afterglow of divine grace in everything, a resonance of primal happiness in creation, for things are yet alert to their Maker, if we but know how to see and listen with them. Eden is but a memory now, yet undying. Every creation conceals a possible plenitude awaiting our complicity to blossom into splendor. But the force that scorns beauty ushers us quickly through creation, ignoring the proffered pleas and offers of pedestrian beauties, momentary companionships, brief communions, fleeting flirtations with things. In our haste we reduce the world to reality and abandon our first duty to expand creation in added dimensions of beauty and significance. We are both mutilated by our neglect: the world is incomplete without our art and thought, and we are bound to it as in love and separated to our sorrow.

Stirring different sensitivities, houses, farms, villages, and cities come into view as I resume my journey and speed along. What would life be like there? What if I lived there? How could I live there? How can I not live there? What forms and degrees of happiness could I have known there? If we are grateful people, we do not regret our life and its allotment of love and time. Yet we know also an ineffable yearning for other lives unlived, faces never seen, friendships forfeited for mortality's brevity, and chances before and beyond our years. The pathways bypassed make full happiness impossible in this world. For happiness to lap the brim we should have to know the lost, bypassed worlds also, have time and heart and patience for them all. Are they reserved in Heaven, the plenitudes of happiness we glimpsed but gainsaid in this world? We speed by some of these possible worlds and cover them with nostalgias of things imperfectly done and little known, and thus set ourselves up for unfavorable comparison to Jesus and the saints who are never hurried, never late, and never fretful. Satan, desperate being that he is, wanders restless like us to and fro about the earth, modeling for us the dark certainty that nothing resembles sin so much as speed.

✝ ✝ ✝

## 31. Separation and Siege

Do these negative principles of the colossal apply to the so-called mega-churches of our time? I leave the question open for the moment, commenting only that mega-churches do not constitute a mega-church. This mega-Protestantism does not have a Pope; it has a hundred. These giant, non-denominational churches usually stand alone, answerable only to themselves and God, some without effective doctrinal and fiscal supervision. Built usually around charismatic personalities, these mega-churches are at considerable risk when the august personages die, which is certain, or go immorally or theologically astray, which is frequent.

Today there are few mysteries left in popular Christianity. For like nearly every dimension of modern life popular Christianity has become loud and extroverted. This is not the world for the timid or contemplative. But here we must ask, is this form of Christianity really possible? Are there not enigmas in Christianity that surpass understanding and must be accepted quietly and humbly on faith? Modern rationalism convinced men that they could explain dimensions of Christianity where rational insight cannot venture. Consequently, most of the modern divisions among Christian branches have come about not over the core but the casuistry. Usually we divide not over deep differences but hairsplitting similarities. For this reason, often Satan will forfeit the great battles in hopes of overcoming us in the marginal skirmishes.

French philosopher Montesquieu wrote that the cure for the ills of the Gallic Church of his day would be to import other sects. Tolerated religious minorities, he explained, normally make themselves more useful and exemplary than the predominant sect. True or not, the presence of many denominations imposes something of a market economy on American Christianity. Because each Christian denomination lives in awareness of and competition with the others and their teachings, it must compete to enhance its image and market its product, so to speak. As a result, most varieties of American Christianity operate only partially at the level of belief and mystery; at the same time it must function at the public level with its confrontational stresses. This makes for great religious effervescence but it can lead to a certain shallowness and doctrinal instability. It can also result in a polemical disposition; there is a general assumption among certain churches that all a denomination needs to do to prove itself right is to prove others wrong.

The embrace of evil is always a Judas kiss of betrayal. Seizing on the Christian impulses of tolerance, forces arising from many sources are converging to undermine, marginalize, and eventually destroy Christianity. Let us not be duped by names; probably there will always be something called Christianity. The question is whether it will have anything to do with Christ and, more, whether Christ will have anything to do with it.

In American society powerful forces are moving against Christianity. Believers think, quite naturally, that wicked people in high places are responsible and rush to oppose them. Of course there are always wicked people in high places who ought to be opposed. But the real story of what is happening in America is more complicated.

A few generations ago the celebrated doctrine "separation of Church and State" became, for better or worse, a juridical principle. But it did not stop there. Less noticeably but more importantly, it soon mutated from the relatively benign intention to separate Church and State into the imperative of expelling Christianity from secular life altogether. The dogma of separation has become the doctrine of elimination. This attempt arose from the public assumption—held by Christians and non-Christians alike—that the secular fell entirely under the purview of the State. In successive stages since the Reformation the Church had come to be narrowly the Church, whereas the State had expanded broadly to include nearly everything else. The modern democratic State is incomparably stronger and more efficient than the puny mechanisms of the old monarchies, and it has extended its reach and control accordingly. During this transformation the principle of separation became a binding social force that commenced to act impersonally, growing in power and spreading beyond its original legal metes and bounds. What began as a juridical realignment took on the character of a social norm endowed with all the power of society we saw earlier. As it stands today, it is less a conspiracy by prominent anti-Christians than the effects of an impersonal social mechanism continuing automatically along a set trajectory. Indeed, many of its human enforcers were—and are—Christians themselves.

Naturally its human enemies have taken advantage of the

tidal movement against Christianity. Yet for the most part, both the defenders and the opponents of Christianity have failed to see that beyond the proposed abolition of Christianity there looms an even bolder ambition, one I will come back to later.

✝✝✝

## 32. America versus the United States

The paragraphs I am about to write disturb me as much as they would any other Christian. But after long consideration it seemed to me that to ignore my forebodings would be to conspire silently with the very thing I dread, even though I was also mindful of the ancient superstition—or is it wisdom?—that to name an evil may help to bring it into being.

If American society continues to drift from its Christian origins, the time may come, and is even now approaching, when believers will have to choose between God and the State, between Christ and what we shall still call America. How heretical the thought, how alien the idea falls on the American mind! For several generations loyalty to faith and flag were so closely tied together that to love and serve one was to love and serve the other as a single, indivisible duty. We are not the first nation to bind our national life to our faith, and if it comes to it, we shall not be the first to have to separate them to our sorrow.

For a different America is forming. A new kind of people is gathering in this land, a people who stand against everything America stood for. They reject American Christianity and scorn the old patriotism, and nothing gladdens them more than to see America defeated. Grim and humorless, they fester with rage and outrage. For them America is not the land of the free but a nation of Christian fools, not the home of the brave but a country of bullies. With practiced indignation they tell us that by right nothing America has belongs to it, but without ethical compunction everything it has they intend to take for themselves or redistribute to the world. In their eyes, nothing is immoral if it serves their cause, and nothing is ethical if it opposes their will. They come from the top and the bottom of America. They are native-born children of pedigree and privilege scornful of their heritage, and they are foreign born come to feed on American generosity yet subversively loyal to cruel cultures that starved their families and stunted their spirits. This other America is not united by language or race or history or religion or culture but by the common cause of demolishing America and recasting it in their various images.

Who, then, will own America? Whose vision will prevail? No one can say, but if the oppositions between the two Americas continue to grow and hatreds mount, a moment will come when tempers overcome tolerance, passions overwhelm patience, bullets replace ballots, and we shall have commenced our second Civil War. Not a war of North and South with clear lines of battle, but of class against class, cause against cause, section against section, race against race, religion against religion: a vast, brutal, disorganized mangling of this democratic land that would surely end in tyranny. Inevitable? No. But no more impossible than the first Civil War seemed to be in 1850. We are not immune; the latest war is never the last war. Shall we forget that Christ looked down the long skein of time and saw wars and rumors of wars until the end of the age?

Let me conclude this dark vision with this summary story. America shares a trait common to many great nations. It consists of a certain historical duality, a double personality. Consider an analogy: in its moments of political and cultural greatness, few countries had more enemies—and more admirers—than France. And in many cases they were the same people. Even as its opponents fought French armies on bloody battlefields, they eagerly awaited the latest word from Paris on art, literature, *haute couture*, and *haute cuisine*. France considered itself to be the home of all fashionable and civilized people everywhere. At different levels, it was often both friend and enemy to its neighbors.

A similar national duality seemed to be prefigured from the beginning by assigning two names to one nation, America and the United States. The case of the United States/America is even more complex than old France, in part due to its colossal dimensions, but it is not only a question of geography but also of two dimensions that are each more complex than anything previous in history. I'll suggest it is two nations occupying the same territory, for I must overstate the point to make it.

In a certain sense, cosmopolitan America belongs superlatively to the whole world. It is an open nation with ethnic and cultural ties to many countries, especially Europe with which it shares a post-Christian secular culture. This America is the second homeland of millions of immigrants.

But of these unnumbered new arrivals relatively few assimilate the unique culture of that other America we call the United States. Most of them are content to live on the fringes—figuratively and geographically—of America, which because of its openness, cosmopolitan attitudes, and ethnic ties is the part they already know and where they can live most conveniently.

Unlike this America, the United States is a relatively closed society characterized by an invincible indifference toward things and people beyond its borders. Scorning the world-wide metric system, for example, it measures its dimensions in miles, feet, and inches, its weights in pounds and ounces; and while the world goes into a collective frenzy over the World Cup, the United States yawns over *fútbol* but thrills to football.

If the foreign policy of this strange, dual nation corresponds to its role as America, its elections are a phenomenon of its alter ego the United States. In reality there are no national elections but fifty state elections, an oddity that befuddles most foreign observers and frustrates no few Americans.

Everyone knows that the newest things in the world come from America, as they once came from France or Great

Britain, but at the same time the United States preserves some of the oldest. The latest slang comes out of New York or Hollywood to infiltrate other languages and spread around the globe, while at a great remove, remnants of Elizabethan English live on in churches and backcountry regions of the United States. Post-Christian culture is predominant in America, while in the United States Christianity not only survives but thrives. Today its temperature is higher and its vital signs much stronger than they were fifty years ago. And the phenomenon has occurred not only in fundamentalist Christianity but also in Catholicism, which almost unnoticed continues to make inroads. This unexpected resurgence, coming at a time when Christianity was expected to die, provokes the post-Christians to angry perplexity. Perhaps the vision that most disturbs post-Christian professors and politicians—and no few liberal theologians—is not Islamic terrorists but a seismic eruption in evangelical Christianity, a prospect some have described as "Christian terrorism."

In our day, three visions of future life compete for supremacy in the world: radical Islam, European-American secular culture, and the resurrected Christianity of the United States. The events of September 11, 2001 effectively began the twenty-first century. On that day the battle was joined and it will be decided—we know not how and to what outcome—where it began: in these not very United States.

†✝†

## 33. A Synopsis of Hostilities

Christianity has never lacked enemies. Mohammed sought to replace it, Marx, to destroy it. For two thousand years its adversaries have warred against it, often as determinedly as today but probably never so fiercely as we shall see tomorrow. And let us be candid: from time to time the foes of Christianity have essentially succeeded. As G. K. Chesterton writes in *The Everlasting Man*, the history of Christianity is the story of its repeated burial and rebirth, as though echoing across the ages the supreme redemptive drama of death and resurrection at Golgatha and Gethsemane.

In the first Christian centuries many people, especially the educated classes, could not understand Christianity. When St. Paul delivered his superbly crafted sermon to the assembled Athenian intellectuals on Mars hill, all but a few ridiculed his talk of an invisible God and the resurrection of a dead savior. Customarily they were eager to hear and dispute every topic imaginable, but these new concepts seemed to violate all reason. They believed themselves to be open-minded but prided themselves on not being empty-headed. Even the Pharisees of Jerusalem, who shared Jesus' Jewish heritage and were close enough to his teachings to dispute with him, did not grasp his radical innovations, much less accept them.

Sophisticated Jews and Greeks alike were also repelled by the lowly status of the followers of the new religion. What merit, they asked scornfully, could there be in a sect that admitted slaves and women and taught them the scandalous doctrine of spiritual equality with their betters?

Also misunderstanding the Christian perspective, the Romans were incensed by what they regarded as treasonous Christian "atheism" in their refusal to worship Caesar. What harm could there be in bowing before Caesar and acknowledging his divinity, they asked, since it was a normal practice in many countries, and the Christian doctrine itself taught that he was appointed by God and deserving of allegiance? But what seemed a formality to the Romans was fundamental to the Christians. This is why they were unwilling to bow for their life but willing to burn for their faith. They rendered unto Caesar all that was Caesar's, but this did not include worship. Nearly three centuries passed before the Romans relented and the martyrdoms ceased.

Today in the Christian heartland of Europe and the

Americas believers need fear no physical persecution for their faith but instead freely enjoy all the secular conveniences. No longer a peculiar people set apart from the world, believers themselves rush to the defense of anti-Christian secularism because of their common cause with unbelievers. After twenty centuries the Roman wish has come true: Caesar and circus, not Christ and *charismata*, claim their first loyalty. Can we not argue that by this unequal alliance Christians themselves have become some of Christianity's worst enemies?

The charges brought against traditional Christianity are many and mounting. Atheists look on the Christian faith as a collection of medieval superstitions, an embarrassing holdover from the Dark Ages of pre-rational gullibility. These are among the most ardent enemies of Christianity, and often their passion to destroy it equals the zeal of the most dedicated evangelists to propagate it. Perhaps this passion is the reason they are also among those most susceptible to conversion. For if they do not believe the same things, they believe with the same intensity as their enemies. Divided, but divided over the same themes, the bitterest of enemies have an odd way of becoming the sweetest of friends.

For assorted camps of deists, otherwise comfortable with an impersonal God—as though a God without personality and passion were somehow superior—Christianity presents a deity discredited because of his obsession with the backwater history of certain Near Eastern desert Semites. Following the lead of eighteenth-century Enlightenment thinkers—Diderot, Condorcet, Voltaire, Gibbon, Hume—they cannot reconcile the God of the Universe with lusty sheepherders, gloomy prophets, fastidious priests, and a vagabond Messiah squabbling over intramural doctrines and threatening divine retributions at the fringes of the ancient Classical world. Surely, they reasoned with Baron d'Holbach, at the very least a rational God would have sent His Son—itself a wildly improbable notion—to be born in Athens, Rome, Alexandria, or one of the other great cities of that age, not in a sleepy Judean village.

Still others who profess belief in Christ also confess distress over the fossilization of dogma and the reluctance of modern Christianity to adjust to the egalitarian culture of our times. Declared guilty without appeal of being a bastion of white male power and privilege and relying too much on ancient, biased texts, certain Christian branches are equally faulted for being a Eurocentric religion reluctant to accommodate women and homosexuals in the pastorate or priesthood. Moreover, assured of its righteous mandate, Christianity doubts—and as often denies—the validity of other faiths and makes only the feeblest attempts to practice the brotherly love and ecumenical tolerance it preaches and which contemporary ethics demand.

But far more contemporary people are indifferent to Christianity, neither opposing nor favoring its teachings. For them the "Good News" is old news and they have long since moved on to other philosophies. For them their fortune in this life trumps their faith in the next. Because they cannot be bothered by Christianity they do not bother with it.

## 34. The Poor Always?

Taken together, the twin intellectual mantras of our day, "post-Christian" and "post-modern," describe a world that, supposedly, has moved past both its Christian heritage and its modern *imperium* of Cartesian/Utilitarian rationalism, colonialism, and canonical art. Only science and its offspring technology remain intact in the general dismantling of Western culture, and even they labor under suspicion and occasional open opposition. As for Christianity, it has been discounted as a thing beyond hope of resuscitation, fit only for the trash bin of history.

The general negativity arising from the deconstruction of the Western world finds one of its strongest expressions in an opposition to human excellence it fostered and the possibility of transcendent immortality it presupposed. Despite the marked material improvements in human welfare in modern times, we rarely hear a good word about mankind, least of all its Christianized branches.

I anticipate an objection. Have I misspoken? Or speak in cruel jest? How dare I talk of "marked material improvements" when every day we hear reports and see images of poverty, disease, and hunger in so many nations of the world?

We can do so responsibly provided we remember—for it seems we have forgotten—that the poor have been with us always, more, that we are all surely descended from poor, diseased, and hungry ancestors. Far from being a modern capitalist conspiracy as our revolutionaries and post-Christians preach, poverty, disease, and hunger were, as far as we know, the normal human condition for thousands of years. The end-time plagues described in *Revelation* not only lie in the apocalyptic future of humanity but also make up woeful chapters of its history. At some unknowable future time the Four Horsemen of the Apocalypse surely will ride out again to devastate mankind, but let us not forget that they have been riding roughshod over the world since the fall of Adam and the loss of Eden. Christ reminded his disciples that they would have the poor always.

It was only when certain portions of mankind—mainly those where Christianity is, or has been preeminent—began to be affluent and healthy that poverty and disease came to be seen not as an unchangeable condition of life but as remediable circumstances. Not until a better way of life at last seemed to be within human reach did these age-old sufferings begin to appear intolerable. It was only when Modern Europeans saw that life could be better that they began the revolutions to demand that it be better. And, paradoxically, the same people whose creativity made a better life possible were blamed later for making it worse.

†✝†

## 35. Christian Guilt, Evolution, and the Universe

Embarrassed in the second half of the twentieth century by their material advances and advantages over other religions and cultures, Christianized peoples convinced themselves that they were to blame for the sorry plight of the world. For if they were healthy and wealthy, as both they and their enemies reasoned, surely it was at the expense of the world's impoverished masses. In the nineteenth century the white Christianized nations believed they had the "burden" of taking Christian civilization to backward lands; in the twentieth the ill-named "third world" countries—and those who manipulated them—accused them of taking everything of value from them.

Darwinism extended this Western sense of guilt to include lower forms of life. In the evolutionary paradigm the human advantage over other animal species seems unfair. As Teilhard de Chardin points out, even if we are willing to accept the general theory of biological evolution, it cannot explain the unique phenomenon of man. Indeed, by Darwinian standards man stands out as a privileged species in the evolutionary panorama. He does not represent the survival of the fittest, but the triumph of the unfit, and, as many would claim today, the undeserving.

Probably no province of science arouses more controversy in Christian groups than Darwinian evolution, which brings us to the question of how to approach it from a Christian perspective.

In order to do justice to any doctrine or science, we should begin by pointing out its truths, that is, by showing the features that make it seem reasonable to enlightened people. And in all cases we should be cautious and careful not to make wishful or dogmatic thinking pass off as reasoned science. And the caveat against close mindedness operates across the spectrum of our imperfect human knowledge. History repeats the humbling lesson that the

THE LIGHT OF EDEN

theories of one age become the jokes of the next.

As for Darwinian evolution, some observations are immediately in order. First, the notion of evolution did not originate with Darwin, Wallace, and Lamarck in the nineteenth century but has an ancient pedigree dating from the early Greek writers, notably Thales, Empedocles, Anaximander, and Epicurus. Aristotle himself suggested a transition between living and nonliving matter, and following the Greeks, the Roman poet Lucretius wrote that "The earth itself created men and animals."

The second observation is that Darwinism is an intellectually engaging theory. Elegantly and broadly crafted, it gracefully accommodates many data from various scientific disciplines. Doubtless it is the best scientific doctrine for its time, and it must remain so for ours unless and until someone can come up with a better one.

The third observation is a cautionary reminder that as Christians and intellectually responsible thinkers, we expose Christianity to grave risk when we bind Christian truth in do-or-die bondage to human theories, even those which appear to support Christianity. Nowhere is this risk greater than when Christians employ such theories to oppose evolution. For should these theories fail, as often they do, by reverse logic it will appear that Christianity has also failed.

Those who oppose Darwinism often base their rejection on the argument that evolutionary theory has dangerous consequences for morality and the Christian faith. But to assume this posture is to place oneself in danger of rejecting truth for the convenience of established ethical protocol. What, then, ought to be the proper Christian attitude toward evolution?

The objections to evolution, which often rest on the best of pious intentions, arise, or so it seems to me, from a faulty anthropology, that is, a flawed theory of man as a human person. Let us, therefore, concede what modern science has demonstrated by countless proofs that convince most informed people, namely, that evolutionary theory tells us what we are as biological beings, as members of the animal world. But it does not explain who we are as persons, much less why we are.

Viewed from this basic dichotomy—which is as simple as it is biblical—we may conclude that Christianity begins where evolution ends and, further, that evolution furnishes indispensable information about our bodily being, which is fundamental to Christianity. Far from threatening or opposing Christianity, therefore, evolution offers us certain basic components in a superior Christian anthropology. Science has done, or is doing its work; now it is time for Christian thinkers to do theirs. Instead of wearying themselves in sterile and strident opposition to evolution, Christian theologians and philosophers should turn it to their advantage, that is, they should accept what man is and flesh out our conceptions of who he is, or may become.

Nothing is more intellectually censurable than to reject science simply because it appears to stand at odds with prevailing religious and moral views. That a scientific doctrine seems dangerous does not mean that is necessarily false.

But as we can find fault with Christian thinking, fairness demands that we not turn a blind eye to the errors of scientific perspectives. In *The Decline of the West*, a book that aroused more admiration than agreement, Oswald Spengler declares that every science is dependent upon a prior religion. If this claim can be taken in an expanded sense to include an adversarial or parasitical dependency, then indeed some of the controversies of modern science find an explanatory context in the notion of divine creation. For modern science has sometimes assumed the twin tasks of pursuing knowledge and repudiating Christianity. If many Christians have erred intellectually by rejecting evolution, some in the scientific camp have made a mistake of similar proportions by trying to turn science into a weapon against Christianity. In both cases, these mistaken attitudes served only to make their opponents appear odious. The result has been that neither side served the cause of truth.

THE LIGHT OF EDEN

A questionable scientific and intellectual opaqueness occurs when certain Christian concepts, among them the creation/Creator hypothesis, are included in the general rejection of Christianity. If the Hebrews had not conceived of a Creator God as a bedrock religious truth thousands of years ago, can we not easily imagine that a scientific theory of this very possibility would be hailed as a brilliant scientific hypothesis? If no one had ever thought of God, how scientifically stunning the theory would be! But religious minds got there first, and nothing is more irritating than truth told by an enemy, especially an enemy one considers to be of inferior intellect.

In any case, there is a strain of modern science that begins not from an objective standpoint—an impossibility in any absolute sense anyhow as we noted in a previous chapter— but from a prior determination to undo and deconstruct the Christian understanding of earth and man as the center stage and showpiece, respectively, of divine creation. One way to accomplish this is to reject creation itself and thus to eliminate the need for a Creator. As physicist Stephen Hawking reasons, in an uncreated or recurring universe where life arises from non-life and science is closing in on "a theory of everything" there will be nothing left for God to do, or theologians and philosophers either, for that matter.

If evolution has proved to be challenge and stimulus to faith, the vastness of the universe chills our spirit. Once we thought that mankind was a special creation residing at the very center of the cosmos. But since Galileo, astronomers have been telling us that our world is not the middle of anything. On the contrary, we learn that our sun is but an insignificant star and earth its mite-sized satellite at the tail end of one of the spiral bands of the Milky Way, itself an inconspicuous galaxy matched and overmatched by billions of others. We are dwarfed by size and intimidated by distance and after all is said and done nothing we are and nothing we do seems to have any final relevance to anything. Puny, insignificant, a speck of cosmic dust, these are the common descriptions of our world and our human condition.

If this understanding of the universe renders moot our moral and religious claims, it also releases us willy-nilly from their protective restraints. Can they be else than empty words, vain whispers swept away in the mindless but mighty spin of the cosmos? Without a Creator and his moral laws, what difference does it make how we live or how we die, what pleasures we seize to our selfishness or pains we inflict to our spite? Not that these bleak thoughts were new; the Bible summarized the existential creed many centuries earlier. As St. Paul wrote, quoting *Isaiah* 22:13, "Let us eat and drink, for tomorrow we die" (*1 Corinthians* 15:32). We shall consider some of these notions in the next chapter.

† † †

## 36. No Exit?

Science and existential philosophy converged in the Modern Age to complete a bleak understanding of human life and its cosmic inconsequence. Leaving aside honest thinkers like Kierkegaard, Unamuno, and Marcel for whom the following comments are not intended, the last cycle of atheistic existential philosophers struggled to establish an ethical foundation for their philosophy. But in vain; everything that Bertrand Russell, Jean-Paul Sartre, Malraux, Camus, and others who thought like them tried to pass off as moral pronouncements on the human condition was transparently at the mercy of relativism. In several cases, their thought was further skewed by a personal devotion to Soviet tyranny. In the end they had no answer to the conclusions reached by science and rendered in their own reasoning: in the grand scheme of things nothing human really matters anyway. In the end Sartre capitulated intellectually by saying that "man is a useless passion." As if he knew; for by his own admission, we can know nothing with absolute certainty.

The later existentialists had reasoned themselves into a

gloomy corner from which, as one of Sartre's titles indicates, there was "no exit," at least not for them. As they saw things, beyond our local freedom and situational ethics looms an alien, uncaring cosmos that smothers all our further hopes. And in its soulless expanse we see reflected our own spiritual emptiness and the utter vanity of human existence. Life, the existentialists concluded, is but a series of flimsy effigies, mere mockeries of all we would hold dear. And the best and worst of our brief worldly run to death are meaningless indulgences in joyless pleasures.

It may seem that I have paid too much attention to a philosophical movement that petered out years ago. I do so precisely for that reason. With existentialism modern philosophy in the traditional European and Western mold reached a dead end. New movements, or at least new names, have arisen or continued-neo-Marxism, structuralism, deconstructionism, chaos theory, and general postmodernist minimalism, to mention but a few—but in every case they avoided, if not scorned, the real metaphysical problems, which are always the problems of real people and real philosophy, and concentrated instead on the important but secondary issues of economics, political agendas, sexist causes, or linguistic word games. With the existentialists modern rationalism had run its course. By declaring beforehand that the age-old concerns of the human condition were both misconstrued and inappropriate, philosophy ceased to consider them at all and limited itself instead to trivial pursuits and linguistic sophistry. Intellectual arteriosclerosis soon set in, and philosophy stagnated, for it lives and is invigorated not so much by the answers it provides as by the radical questions it raises.

Is this, then, the end of the human story? Does the decline of post-existential philosophy reflect the fate of humanity? Is there really no way out? Can there be no rebuttal to Galileo and his scientific descendants or to Sartre and his existential ilk, all of whom have taken pains to deconstruct human uniqueness and deny our transcendent hopes?

Christian believers customarily respond, of course, that

by faith they will be rescued from this inconsequential world and raised to a higher destiny. Beyond the bleak nihilism on which modern rationalism ultimately founders, the Christian points to the great biblical promises of redemption and eternal life.

But this approach makes sense only to those who accept the authenticity of the Christian faith, the Church, and the validity of the Scriptures. It does no good to appeal to Christ, Church authority, or biblical chapter and verse to those who reject Christ, the Church, and the Bible *ab initio*, from the start. Without calling it by its medieval name, their dismissal amounts to the strategy of *nego suppositum* (I deny the assumption), which consists in this instance of rejecting the premise that the Christian Bible is a valid and truthful document and, in the case of Catholic believers, that the Church is invested with divine authority and binding tradition. This tactic effectively thwarts and frustrates many Christians who are unable to argue outside these twin premises. Consequently, it often happens that in these encounters frustrations rise, reciprocal anathemas may be pronounced, and the communication that never was can then never be. In these cases, a different strategy is called for. In the last section of this book I shall suggest another approach by reasoning in an entirely different way, a Christian way, about our human condition and circumstances.

# VI

## HISTORY AND HUMAN DESTINY

American philosopher George Santayana made the celebrated statement that those who forget their history are
doomed to repeat it. But Cicero may have been closer to the
truth two thousand years earlier when he wrote that as long
as men are ignorant of the past they remain children.

✝✝✝

### 37. History, Nature, and Artificial Man

If Cicero was right, ignorant men are children without
real childhood. The world they know is dangerous and
unforgiving, whereas in authentic childhood it appears to
suspend its harshness and accompany us for a short time in
revisited innocence. Children are privileged to hear faint
echoes of happy Eden. Wordsworth says in *Intimations of
Immortality*:

> *But trailing clouds of glory do we come*
> *From God, who is our home:*
> *Heaven lies about us in our infancy!*

And Christian poet Thomas Traherne seconds the
thought in *Wonder*:

> *How like an angel came I down!*
> *How bright are all things here!*

But the world's childish condescension is limited; eventually it sloughs off its youthful mask, as a serpent sheds its

skin, and shows us its ugly gashes and ghastly scars. Our childish illusions melt away in the realization that our dreams have been dreamt before us, our games already played, our joys known of old. Thus does the early exuberance of life pass from the world and only reflective contentment remains. For the happiness that flows from mature wisdom is forged in meditation and refined by limits and renunciations.

Santayana's pronouncement sounds ominous, but were it literally true, would not many people risk reliving their life so as to make better choices the next time around? There are stories of second chances in various literatures, but they are always tales of failure. For life has a rhythm that assigns a due time to its stages, and if there is any sort of fatalism at work in human matters, it is in their timing. As the Bible says, there is a time and a season for all things, and its lesson for us is that to live out of pace with life's seasonal cycle is to reduce our acts to futility or exaggerate them to parody. Our seasons come in their course and are gone. In the nests of yesteryear, writes Cervantes, no birds remain today.

To go a step beyond Cicero and Santayana, it is even truer that those who forget their history forfeit their future. According to Montesquieu and Benjamin Franklin, happy is the country that has no history. The only thing wrong with their observation is that so such country exists. To be human is to be historical. Without history we, like man in nature, would find ourselves trapped in an everlasting past. For primitive mankind the trouble with the past is that it does not pass, and this means that savage life is a perpetual anachronism, a childhood that grows to old age without growing up, humanity to be sure but of a lower sort sensible only to lesser gods.

As we saw earlier, the notion that savage mankind is more genuinely human than civilized man is a modern fallacy that has blighted Western science and art since Rousseau and the Enlightenment. Far from being nature's pet, as Rousseau taught and Gauguin painted, primitive man is its victim, ensnared in its timeless trap like a fly caught in a spider's web. The perceived charms of primitive life are myopic distortions peculiar to the Christianized West and must not be confused with the Classical love of bucolic life. An abyss exists between Horace's praise of orderly country life on his Sabine farm and the modern infatuation with savage nature. Perhaps tucked away in the recesses of our psyche we retain some ancient folk recollection of primitive life, as the psychologists of the unconscious used to tell us. But if so, it is a treacherous memory, for time performs its usual trickery on far memories: pains evaporate and pleasures exaggerate.

Nature and the natural have had centuries of good press, probably because there is a lingering belief that it is closer to God's original creation. On the other hand, the artificial sounds contrived and false to our modern ears. If we can find them, we prefer natural remedies for our physical ailments and seek natural scenery for spiritual healing. The delusion has spread among modern people that our problems began when human kind left nature. Yet our humanity cannot prosper in the natural state but depends instead on the very artificiality we scorn in modern times. Expulsion from Eden was a mandate to build civilization. We live humanly not by instinct or natural strength but by the enhancement and multiplication of our powers through education, art, and technology. To state it in purely zoological terms, man is the animal who cannot live as an animal.

If natural life confines us to the possible, education and art allow us to live the impossible life. In nature we cannot fly like a bird, run like a deer, or swim like a fish. We can only pretend to do so, as primitive peoples do in their rituals. Furthermore, in our native state we are either a man or a woman and, naturally speaking, cannot experience human life in its other dimension we call the other sex. Not only this but we are born and spend our mortal years confined to a certain era and culture unable to know life as, randomly, an ancient Egyptian, medieval monk, Chinese noblewoman, Scythian warrior, first-century Jew, or arctic Inuit.

Artificially our fate is quite different. By means of our manmade artifacts we are enabled to soar higher than the eagle, outrace the cheetah, and out swim the shark. And as the quintessence of artificiality, art surpasses technology by permitting an even more fabulous expansion of our life. It allows us virtually to transcend the limitations of sex, culture, and time. Through art we can visit lands out of sight and know people—real or fictional—impossibly beyond the reach of our natural experience. Earlier I referred to the "sympathy of circumstances," which allows us to bond with the lives and loves of men and women in ages and lands distant from ours. Without art in its multiple forms we would be diminished to an impoverished "natural" life unable to transcend our brief time and place. Art is the art of being human.

The revelatory power of art applies not only to things beyond our life but also to realities within it. It illuminates not only the far reaches of human experience but the hidden mysteries and beauties of our own being. All reality is enigmatic and none more so than the radical reality of our own life, which is the first encountered and usually the last understood.

Yet we must remember that the human story does not end even with these great privileges. Our ultimate calling does not stop with the natural, nor the artificial, nor yet the artistic, but with the eternal. If through art and technology we can discover and master both the world's real and unreal dimensions, by God's grace we shall transcend these also and live a divine life. Could this be the ultimate meaning of Jesus' enigmatic reminder to the Pharisees: "Is it not written in your law, 'I said, Ye are gods?'" (*St. John* 10:34).

History, itself an art and the most human of all, fulfills its main function by freeing us from the past. The past is the condition of the present and the parent of the future, but it is tyrannical and does not easily release us. It must be domesticated as history lest it usurp the present and abort the future.

Human history, like human faith, comes in two forms:

one living, the other dead. The deceased version lies moldering in the tombs we variously call archives, tomes, and museums; the living variety resounds in markets and along Main Street in what the poet Milton called "the busy hum of men." And the din reminds us that, written or not, history is not what died and passed away but what survived and remains alive today. As historian R. J. Collingwood observes, history books begin and end, but the events they describe do not.

To dead history we owe the respectful acknowledgment due all human things done in by mortality, but to living history we direct our earthly enthusiasms and hopes. The history that interests us here has little to do with the chronicles of things that died and much with those that survived. As we shall see later, in Christianity history lives out its most transcendent form of survival, but in ways not always clearly understood.

Approaching history from racist and sexist perspectives in recent years, professional historians have debated about the rightful "owners" of history, implying with particular reference to American history that groups once denied their rightful place in national history can now seek redress. From our standpoint this impulse is more naïve than noble. Dead history can belong to anyone who wishes to claim its cadaver, but living history lives in us all, and we in it.

Modern psychologists make the assumption that we possess a quality or set of qualities called "human nature" which can be studied and categorized. In daily conversation we speak of this nature as though it were a fact and offer it as a convenient explanation or excuse for all forms of behavior, especially our undesirable acts. If not animal instinct, human nature is a close relative. It may also be that we share a common human nature, as psychologists understand the term, though they have yet to make a convincing case for it. But it is much more apparent that we have a human history, or to summarize it better, we are our history.

Yet even if we take the latter view, we should not make the mistake of thinking that we are nothing but our history and so stagnate in reactionary historicism, which is contrary to the movement of history itself. Besides our historical reality we must acknowledge other components of our life, foremost among them our futuristic life calling with its amorous, vocational, and eternal dimensions. And it is the quality of our response to this calling that defines our life. Even though this calling is conditioned by history and limited by the possibilities it offers in each era, it is nonetheless mysteriously personal. Clearly we are called, but considering the matter from a purely worldly perspective we do not know the source of the summoning voice.

It is ironic that even as historians like Gibbon and Voltaire elevated history above the level of dynastic chronicles and created the ancestral versions of modern historiography, they also removed the divine plan from the human story. In the end history lost in form what it gained in format. By divesting history of its divine plot, skeptical historians extended its scope even as they lost its unifying purpose. Instead of working toward the climax of the human story, history became the documented but directionless account of calamities, injustices, sufferings, and outrages. It ceased to be anecdote only to become absurdity. It would be interesting to investigate the links between the skeptical theory of historiography and the rise of the irrational existential doctrines.

I have added the adjective "human" to the living history that concerns us here in order to distinguish it from other kinds of history, most prominent among them "natural history," the collective name for those branches of science that deal with zoological, botanical, and mineral categories. The distinction is fundamental if, as I have come to suspect, "natural history" is based on an erroneous understanding of human history.

Human history is a vastly more complex reality than so-called natural history. Human history displays a double-planed temporal depth marked at both levels by beginnings, vicissitudes, plentitudes, and finalities. First, we were born into a preexisting historical and social world which I have just called "living history." It transcends us in time and scope and exerts countless pressures on our private life, as we saw in our brief sketch of social reality in an earlier chapter. Second, within that larger world we shape our personal life with its peculiar biographical channels, accidents, tendencies, dissensions, and temporal markers.

✝✝✝

## 38. History and the Flopping Fish

If we had never seen a fish and came upon one flopping on a riverbank, we might very well reason logically that its movements were purposeless and inexplicable. Without knowing the fish's history, how it came to be on the bank, and the normal circumstances of its life, we might conclude that its actions served no rationally discernible purpose and were patently absurd. But if we learn that fish live in water, that the fish we see flopping was caught by a fisherman, and that its movements are a desperate effort to return to its lifesaving element, then its actions make pathetic sense.

Likewise, if we see an enraged man screaming and waving his arms at a dog we may take him for a madman until we learn that the dog dug up his favorite flowerbed and that on several earlier occasions destroyed other plants in the man's yard. Once we know the history of these unhappy antecedents, his actions and his anger become understandable.

We understand the actions of people and the course of events only when we see them emerge from a prior situation, and that situation in turn from an earlier one, and so on in regression. History is a story, a true story of how things came to be as they are. It is knowledge set in its real temporal depth. Curiously enough, the modern science of psychoanalysis made a similar discovery: the patients' biographical narratives contained the cause of, and perhaps the cure for, their neuroses.

On the other hand, the seventeenth-century Cartesian rationalists thought reason alone was sufficient to enlighten mankind about reality. Descartes himself led off by stating that reason or good sense (*bon sens*), as he called it, was a universal quality and a sure means of discerning truth and falsehood. His followers soon reasoned that by means of rationality Adam, or anyone since, had the same access to knowledge and truth as they did. Following this line of thought to the exclusion of other methods, they reached the certainty that many things did not make "good sense" and indeed were irrational. A century later, in the Enlightenment, Christianity was included among them.

But for all its admirable efficiency, pure rationalism considers primarily—I was about to say only—what is visible and evident, that is, facts or data. It takes note of the flopping fish or the angry man we saw but not the reasons why they act as they do, for those reasons are rooted in time and are not readily visible. Rationalism operates on the surface of reality as though it had no depth and considers it as it is now but not how it came to be as it is. In short, it chooses not to consider things in their history. It gives reasonable accounts of things and events in their present configurations, but not the reasons why they came to have those configurations.

Here the problem we shall address begins to take shape. Nothing human is mere fact or datum. There is much more to an event than the moment of its occurrence. Indeed, a full understanding of any event is utopian, for its concatenation with prior realities would take us all the way back to the beginning of creation. On the basis of available rational evidence the rationalist would—and does—consign us to our evident biology, but in order to understand anything truly human we must narrate a story of how we came to be who we are and not just what we are. We are biological creatures but beyond that we are biographical persons.

What I have just said veers in step with the Bible. In large measure it consists of narratives about human and divine persons. The teachings of Jesus, for instance, were not set down as abstract, rationalistic compilations of laws and principles. Jesus was not a rationalist, which is a way of saying he was much more than a rationalist. He did not write books and treatises but taught by doing, or better, by living, and as a part of his life, by dying and rising to life again. He did not describe the Way or point to it in the manner of a sage or a wise man, but declared that he is the Way. And he revealed himself as the Way one step at a time in the unfolding of his life. His truth cannot be abstracted from who he is. His words cannot be separated from the Word.

Written or oral history has always been a story of what happened. And the fact that we are able to tell it is additional evidence that history continues to be a part of our reality. But in recent times the proliferation of documents and the accumulation of information available to the historian has infringed on the narration of history, threatening to convert it into a massive documentary rather than a narrative. Facts alone are not history and certainly not truth. The historian sometimes finds that he is too overwhelmed with facts to tell the story. Think, for instance, of the mountains of papers housed in each contemporary American ex-president's library. As Charles Péguy once noted, it is impossible to write ancient history because we lack sources, and impossible to write modern history because we have too many. There is but one constant: every generation believes it has lived through the world's most critical age and witnessed its most important changes. In retrospect we are amused at what they took so seriously, especially themselves, for problems that have been resolved lose their drama and fade into the ordinary. But if we belittle those who have preceded us we set an example for those who will belittle us. In any case, history's resolutions should not be mistaken for solutions. When problems are upon us we deal with them as best we can, but then time sweeps them away and sets before us a more urgent agenda. History is always a story that ended unfinished.

I insisted earlier that we are our history. But if true, how is it true? To begin with, we have to discount, or at least relegate to a secondary plane, the common notions that our history can be described in political, social, economic, or cultural terms, the usual funnels into which we pour the interpretations of our time. If we are our history then it has an anthropological dimension and cannot be understood from these secondary categories. To be human is to be historical, and as we saw, to the degree that men lack history their humanity is diminished. Furthermore, if history is the reason why we have come to be as we are, then compared to rationalism it must be seen as a higher form of reason. Unlike abstract rationalism which operates on the factual plane of reality, historical reason alone is able to explain human reality in its temporal depth. It does not accept facts as mere facts but considers them in their contextual depth in order to see how they became facts in the first place. Those who insist on the facts only will discover sooner or later that they are always after the fact.

Not that rationality and history lead necessarily to antagonistic forms of reason. The mistake the rationalists made was not in extolling abstract reason but in trying to impose it on a broader and much more inclusive form of reason. Instead, what Kant called "pure reason" must be viewed as a subset of historical reason, as a star must be understood as part of a galaxy.

When we say that human life is anthropologically historical, that is, that historicity is an ineradicable component of life, we are also saying that historical reason cannot be extraneous to life, that it is not simply instrumental but constitutive. To put it in bolder terms, we must conclude with Ortega that life itself is reason. The rationalistic historians and philosophers complained that history did not make sense, and they were right: life does not make sense; it is sense. If modern philosophy, and especially the existential varieties deriving from Cartesianism, pronounced human life to be pointless and absurd, it was because their version of rationality was instrumentally inadequate. It was

like trying to take the measure of a whale with a micro-
scope.

Here we need to connect this historical reason to the
projective, futuristic, or "facial" character of human life
discussed in an earlier chapter. Historical reason does not
come to light in the abstract, especially not in the light of
abstract reasons, but only within a context of real human
decisions and initiatives. It presupposes human freedom, or
to put it another way, without freedom there would be no
history. The so-called "natural" history of a stone, for
instance, has almost nothing in common with human
history arising from human decisions and acts. The illumination human history offers in the form of understanding
becomes evident only when we examine actual events. Only
when we know what options people had can we understand the ways they chose and why they rejected certain
alternatives, wisely or unwisely as the case may be. And
these options become clear only when we hear their narrative, only when we tell their story.

But whichever the path people have taken, understanding also imposes on us the obligation to determine as
far as possible the degree of human engagement. At times
societies and individuals commit themselves with brimming enthusiasm to a new historical direction—a war, a
conquest, a social reorganization, a different economic
order—on other occasions, only half-heartedly with many
misgivings and internal dissensions. Furthermore, some
rejected options disappear immediately from the social
horizon; others remain as lingering temptations, phantoms
that will not quite die. To put what I have just said in other
words, history is the story of human projects of varying
magnitude, intensity, commitment, success, failure, and
second guessing.

I said that history always ends as an unfinished story.
And the reason is the future is its final dimension. With this
in mind we see that it is not simply a matter of recounting
the past but rather of telling about the futuristic projects of
which human life consists in the first place. This is what

gives history its dramatic movement. The intelligence, richness, and poverty of these projects allow us to take the measure, intensity, and authenticity of human life in each era. At times the drama is weak and barely arouses our interest, at others, powerful and suspenseful. On a national level, some countries have an engaging history that lasts for centuries, while others stagnate in mediocrity during their entire collective life. This is not to say that such countries have no history, only that it does not capture our attention or deserve our admiration.

Like all human things, living history is subject to tempting deviations. In our day exaggerated nationalisms, religious fanaticisms, and various ideological or racial models are constant threats to distort or supplant it. This is a way of saying that secondary realities may disrupt or even usurp the human narrative. When this happens, historical reason declines, leaving the door open to various historical fictions. Whole eras of humanity have lived in delusional dead ends. We may be in such a time.

† † †

### 39. Sexuate History and the Insider Doctrine

History has nearly always been told and understood from a masculine point of view. Yet I claimed in an earlier chapter that the sexes live in a dynamic relationship of shifting balances and adjustments. According to the biblical story of creation, neither sex was inherently superior or inferior to the other. What affects one immediately affects the other; when one shifts the other shifts as when a couple dances, and the more smoothly they adjust to each other the smoother and more enjoyable their dance will be. In recent times in Western societies the sexes have danced awkwardly and uncertainly, but this is far from proof that the sexuate dance of life is over and that the sexes have taken up hostile positions. But the question remains, why has the masculine viewpoint almost always prevailed historically?

Psychologist Alfred Adler claimed that "masculine dominance is not a natural thing," and generations of feminists have repeated his thought so often and forcefully that it has become a popular social theorem. The Bible relates it to the fall of mankind. In the nineteenth century French novelist Georges Sand suggested that one way men subjugated women was to burden them with chastity. "The virtue of woman," she wrote accusingly, "is a fine invention of man." Perhaps it would be closer to the truth and in line with my earlier assertions about the sexes to say that each is the invention of the other. Each comes to know itself only in dynamic reference to the other. No woman would define herself as a woman if there were only women in the world, and the same can be said of men.

Here it helps also, or so I think, to draw a line between "official" and "real" history, which to some extent—though not entirely—duplicates the "dead" and "living" history outlined earlier. Although this official history may concentrate on the deeds of men, and preferentially on the dynasties and wars of kings and governments, "living" history includes the undocumented story of life in its intimate, daily configurations of home, market, church, and neighborhood where women often have a decisive role. To humble daily history philosopher Unamuno gave the apt name of "intra-history." Unlike the dramatic but disjunctive triumphs and tragedies of wars, dynasties, empires, leaders, and national rivalries, "intra-history" continues in its steady, unbroken skein from mother to daughter, father to son, day to day, year to year, generation to generation, and age to age. Without calling it by name, modern historians also discovered this foundational dimension of human life and elevated it to full historiographical dignity. Thanks to them the chronicles of kings includes the history of commoners, and the history of men is also the story of women.

The fact remains, however, that in earlier centuries to be a woman in a man's world meant that even though not numerically in the minority, she had to live with the greater awareness and more stringent rules common to minorities. Perhaps this is the main reason why in recent decades she has made her case with them.

Neo-Thomist philosopher Jacques Maritain wrote that the Middle Ages was both humble and magnanimous, but he and others who extol the medieval centuries—and I count myself among them—may have overlooked certain aspects of feminine life that were perhaps more humiliating than humble. While the Bible itself is generally even-handed in its treatment of women, especially the New Testament, medieval theologians sometimes pointed to woman as the source of evil. Eve of the Bible and Helen of Troy, for example, supposedly demonstrated how women could bring misfortune to whole peoples and races. "Womanly folly" was even an argument in legal cases. No wonder, then, as Montaigne observed: "Women are not altogether in the wrong when they refuse the rules of life prescribed to the World, for men only have established them and without their consent."

To be even handed with the Middle Ages, however, it is important to point out that even as some women were condemned unfairly for their troublemaking, others were adored unreasonably for their charms. The whole cycle of chivalry presupposed that the noble courage of knights and the worshipful gallantry of lovers devolved on the ideal of the fair lady in whose honor men sought to do daring deeds and sing beautiful songs. Woman was subject to a dual destiny in that strange age: either to be put on trial or on pedestals.

Compared to man, woman lived in a different relationship to the social order of earlier centuries, and for this reason it makes sense that her logical premises would be different. Nothing would be more unreasonable than for woman to reason like man if she could not live like him. If today the differences between masculine and feminine reasoning appear to be diminishing, it is probably because their respective ways of life have converged to some degree.

THE LIGHT OF EDEN

Woman tends to think more like man because now she lives more like him.

Nevertheless, this sexuate convergence cannot be complete. Unisex may apply to restrooms and haircuts but not to the wider spectrum of human reality. This means that if it exists at all, a uniform "human nature," which we saw earlier, is still an unusable abstraction. A more promising approach would be to follow common experience which recognizes two "natures": male and female. Exasperated Professor Higgins wonders in *My Fair Lady* why a woman cannot be like a man. To which we can only answer simplistically, because she is a woman who acts out of her womanly condition.

This being said, the legendary male perplexity over woman's unique logic may contain a kernel of truth but likely an even greater amount of comic exaggeration. It is a lighthearted, conventional falsehood of Western societies for men to say they cannot understand women. But a deep human need of both sexes obliges them to do just the opposite. The normal, socially adjusted man shows his understanding of women every day in harmonious relationships, unlike the failed man who really misunderstands women, who bores or frightens them, and who cannot win their friendship or trust, least of all their love.

If traditionally men have exaggerated the puzzling nature of feminine logic, women have tended to simplify male reasoning by casting it into predictable, generic categories. Historically, men have written and speculated much about women, sometimes pejoratively as in the case of misogynists John Knox the theologian or Arthur Schopenhauer the philosopher, but more often adoringly as in the case of the Minnesingers, chivalric bards, and generations of their Romantic descendants.

In contrast, women have said comparatively little about men—as much as they deserve, the misanthropist feminist might add. But perhaps not as much as woman herself needs to know if her common failure to anticipate what man will do is any measure of her judgment. It is true that man

*VI / History and Human Destiny* 151

often lazily lives down to the clichés about him because he knows it amounts to an effortless conformity. But he is just as prone to more energetic impulses of which he may give—or have himself—little advance warning. The high level of feminine—and human—misery in our time suggests that woman's pat assumptions about man are as often wrong as right. Woman probably knows herself better than man knows himself, for she is much more conscious of her body and her immediate circumstances. She communes with the world through her senses, whereas man configures reality to his prior conceptions. Someone has said that man does not fall in love with a woman but with the image he has created of her. Every man seems to have a theory about things regardless of his knowledge or ignorance of them. For these reasons most likely both sexes would benefit if woman would dedicate more of her perceptive powers to uncovering and releasing the secrets of masculine life. For man is gifted in taking the measure of reality, less so in knowing about himself.

We come to a negative point. In recent decades what sociologist Robert Merton calls the "Insider Doctrine" has placed restrictions on intersexuate freedom of the sexes to talk about each other. But the taboo extends further: insiders of nearly every sect, group, ethnicity, race, and inverted sex have embraced the notion that only they can understand their group and that no outsider can or should speak for them. Women, the theory says, must speak exclusively for women; only members of given ethnicities and races have the right to speak for their group, and the subsexes also have their inviolable territory.

The premise of the Insider Doctrine was poorly reasoned to begin with, and its logic quickly peters out in absurdities. To begin with an error is to end with a greater one. By its logic no one living today could have any reliable knowledge of medieval Frenchmen or biblical Hebrews, or for that matter, Elizabethan English folk. For none of us belongs to those civilizations. To adhere strictly to the Insider Doctrine artists, writers, and ultimately scholars as well, would be confined to the purely local events of their time, sex, and place.

But human things are too important to be left solely to insiders. The Insider Doctrine is the latest example of how political and ideological activism and its ugly stepchild political correctness have usurped aesthetics, art, and philosophy in modern times. Much of what passes for literature in our day is open or thinly concealed ideological propaganda and agenda, which is probably one reason why it is everywhere in decline. Political reality is important, political oppression urgent, but they pass over our life like a storm over a flower garden and are gone, leaving the deeper realities and problems agitated but intact.

If the "Insider Doctrine" permits gated access only to the exclusive few, authentic art and humanistic curiosity may be understood as an "Outsider Doctrine," which opens the gates to any person to speak of any group or person in any age. It presupposes not only the rare ability to transmigrate artistically to other human states, genders, times, and conditions but also the capacity for astonishment over the overlooked, ordinary features of life which permits the artist to see through the blinding familiarity of things and bring to light unsuspected beauties and further dimensions of truth. Its validity lies in the fact that no single perspective exhausts the possibilities of creation, and none has the moral right to prohibit others provided they are genuine. Every genuine artistic perspective is an irreplaceable vision of the world, and this essential complementarity begins with the unique views that men and women of every race, group, or ethnicity bring to bear on one another.

✝✝✝

40. A Matter of Time and the Question of Generations

In this world human life, like human history, is inseparable from time yet irreducible to it. On the personal plane we say that time passes, at a geological crawl in childhood, with runaway acceleration in old age. We attribute this perceived change in temporal speed to a mysterious sensorial flaw in ourselves. For surely the pace of time is always the same. Or is it? Is it not conceivable that time accelerates relative to our personal situation within it? Is time absolute or relative? Is it obedient to clocks and calendars, or do they fail to mark its vital pace? Could we not theorize on experience alone—though always beggared for definitive proof—that the personal acceleration of time is a species of relativity similar to the material relativity in Einstein's theories? The Universe is marvelously pliable and has a way of accommodating itself circumstantially to our life. It appears as grimy or grandiose, as bright or blemished, as we are. Our understanding of the world is made in our own image. Tell me what you think of the world and I will tell you who you are. The more we learn about creation the more splendid and mysterious it turns out to be. The German philosopher Hegel suggested that whatever man can imagine is possible and, what is more, will come to pass. Surely this is an exquisite bit of Teutonic exaggeration though not without its usual germ of truth. As Ortega once quipped, in Hegel's time it appeared that half of Germany preferred to get drunk on beer; the other half on intoxicating ideas.

In any case, the faster time goes by the more it lodges in a particular way in human life. Otherwise, how could we think of age as a personal quality or possession? By virtue of time we live, and by excess of time we die. Paradoxically, we run out of time because we have accumulated too much of it. Just when we have too much we have too little. "Old and full of days" is an illuminating biblical description of life's final earthly stage when men like Abraham, Isaac, and Jacob stagger and collapse under the temporal weight of years as though bearing them on their back.

A problematic series of questions arises when we attribute age and years to things. Perhaps imputing a familiar and personal quality to the world is a primary way of humanizing it, but it remains questionable whether this numerically tagged temporal dimension, which arises from human experience and is, therefore, thoroughly subjective in origin, can also be an objective and impersonal means of measuring reality. We spoke in an earlier chapter of the final impossibility of absolute objectivity. Perhaps nowhere does this become more evident than in dealing with time and the so-called objective world.

It is debatable and ultimately unknowable, therefore, whether inanimate realities exist in time the same way we live in it. Intuitively we sense a difference; experientially we see it with our eyes, and common language makes a distinction. With animals we observe the growth, decline, and end of their life and by analogy hypothesize an experience similar to ours. Furthermore, higher animals in close proximity to humans often exhibit fascinating and sometimes disturbing "humanlike" behavior. Yet their acquired behavior is much more deficient than their adoring masters care to admit. Animals, for instance, do not live in history and without historical memory there can be no real identity in the personal sense. If we do not know where we come from, we do not know who we are or where we are going, or at least why we are going. Animals can be humanlike but they cannot be persons, and the separation is abyssal. But do not the same limitations apply to many people? Indeed so; as I wrote earlier, humanity admits of degrees of personhood. If God is a person, as Christian theology plainly teaches, dare we say that the only complete person is God Himself?

Whether or not time flows uniformly beyond human life may be finally unknowable, but we do know that in human history it does not. Instead it proceeds in stages we call generations. "One generation passeth away and another generation cometh," says the writer of *Ecclesiastes*, repeating a human perception as old as humanity.

Historical time, then, is articulated in segments, or steps, in the manner of a walking person or an animal. Without going far astray, we could say that history moves not as an ever-flowing river of time—a common but misleading metaphor—but by discontinuous generations that could be studied, measured, and profiled. But here it is important to understand that we do not complete a step before beginning the next. Analogously, the historical stage is never occupied by a single generation but by several in various stages of preparation, ascendancy, predominance, and decline. And thus humanity moves on in its mysterious journey.

This means that each generation is a unique human grouping. Persons in old photographs and portraits, for instance, strike us not only as old in time but different in type. We may find physical or racial features similar to ours in our ancestors, but if we are honest about it, we also sense in them a baffling strangeness—a gesture, a look, an emotion—that resists our full understanding. They look like us and yet do not seem like us. And this perplexity reminds us how indelibly our time and place mark our generation in turn. Some blind weakness or exceptional virtue binds us unmistakably to our generation. If certain persons are gifted to see beyond their age, their foresight presupposes also the context of their time, else it would not be foresight in the first place. If time travel were possible, it might prove to be unbearable to the traveler, not because he would alter the balance of the world and unwittingly destroy the very conditions of his life, as science fiction authors write, but because it would transport him to a generational time tragically beyond his spiritual tolerances. In any case, our life is here and now, and probably a good thing, too.

It would take us too far afield even for the broad parameters of this book to scan the surprisingly few serious studies of generations theory. The best I have seen is the book by Julián Marías, *Generations: A Historical Method*, although studies by Leopold van Ranke, François Mentré, and Ottokar Lorenz, among a few others, deserve attention. Everybody talks about generations but comparatively speaking very few have tried to turn notion into a rigorous concept.

Here it is worth noting that the generational march of

history appears to be consistent in related cultures. Stated in a better way, the generational coordination is a prime component of their relationship. If we take a certain date in Western history, say 1860, we find not only a synchronous chronological rhythm but also a shared fund of suppositions, enthusiasms, problems, personalities, fashions, philosophies, and trends that set the tone and tempo of that era. They established a general level whereby people could measure themselves and sense whether they were up to date or behind the times. What we loosely call "world opinion" is generally a certain level of shared expectations among kindred cultures.

It is not that these common themes and passions necessarily make for concord. This fallacious assumption is often used to discredit the generations theory. Instead, they lead as readily to discord, even war. As an example, in 1860 Americans were deeply divided but over the same problems, especially the matter of slavery. We could say they were antagonistically embraced like two wrestlers. On the other hand, they had no discernible differences concerning abortion or homosexuality, for these were not the defining generational issues of that era.

All I have said here applies to people belonging to certain species of civilization and not to alien, a-historical, or prehistoric cultures. Indeed, the points made would have to be reversed in the case of primitive human life. Beyond simple biological succession, the generational movement of history as I described it earlier does not seem to occur in such cultures because there is no history to move in the first place.

Nearer at hand and much more problematic is the matter of generational disconnects between contiguous, interactive cultures arising from different historical origins. To give an extreme example, when Columbus discovered, or encountered the Native American cultures, by no stretch of the calendar could it be said that the Europeans and the Americans were living in the same time or that their generational series matched. In our own day and with as many individual exceptions as one might wish to cite, similar arguments could be made about Western and Islamic peoples. They live in different eras with a different generational series. For this reason, it is futile, not to say irresponsible and dangerous, to make the sort of assumptions that Americans could reasonably make about Frenchmen, Englishmen, Italians, or Germans with whom they share a general Western culture and a similar generational sequence. As for Islam and the West, East is East and West is West, but it is not that the twain shall never meet, as Kipling wrote, for they are met to their mutual tragedy.

# VII

## A CHRISTIAN WORLDVIEW

Nothing human is alien to Christ and nothing alien to Christ is human.

† † †

### 41. The Church Inside and Out

All we have said about history remains valid, but now we are ready to approach human history from a different perspective that will require us to move to a higher level of understanding. We begin by going to church.

What do we see and sense when we enter a church building for the mass or service? The obvious of course: congregants or parishioners, pastors, priests, or bishops, prayer, scriptural readings, a reverent mood, music and hymns, homilies or sermons, in liturgical churches perhaps incense, iconic symbols, and the culminating Eucharist, in more puritanical churches the lack of these signs which nevertheless are yet silently present by their very absence. Thus we experience all the familiar yet mysterious stages of worship, and, not least, what may seem a welcome respite from the world and its problems. We find comfort—and for some, comfortable boredom—in the elements and phases of corporate worship.

But if we meditate on the messages and probe beyond these initial appearances a larger image begins to take shape. We come to realize that there is more inside the Church than outside in the world. We enter the restricted

space of the Church sanctuary and discover a larger world
than the one we left at its door. For despite its immensity
and complexity, the outside world, the so-called "real
world," is neither wholly real nor fully complete. Its history
is not the whole of history; our secular life is not a complete
life. On the other hand, far from excluding the world and
sequestering us for a brief time in a sanctuary, the Church
claims a peculiar custody over all human history. In it are
deposited—perhaps without its express knowledge—the
richness, error, suffering, and wisdom of all human
endeavor. The Church is heir to the entire history of
mankind past and yet to come. It embraces the story of
humanity beginning with Adam and Eve and includes the
dispersal of peoples, the wanderings of Abraham, the rise
and razing of kingdoms, the names of humble men and
women, and the unnamed peoples who migrated
unrecorded to the ends of the earth. The pious and the
pagan, the godly and the ungodly, all come under the
Church's motherly purview, for the Church is feminine in all
languages but English. She recognizes all her children, and
her children are all who have been or will be born into this
world. They may not confess God and believe in his Church
but we know that God loves them and his Church believes
in them, even if they do not have faith in themselves.

We do not—or should not—turn our back on the world
when we enter a church. Far from it; we go there—and the
going is both a physical and spiritual movement—not only
to reconnect with the spiritual world but also to this world,
to acknowledge the fullness and folly of this plane of life,
the entirety of its good and evil, and to contemplate its total
redemption. This is why churches that incline preferentially
to certain ethnic or national groups and cling preferentially
to certain times or stages of history—the primal beginnings
of Christianity, for instance—fall short of the church's
universal vision. The true Church can have no national,
temporal, or cultural boundaries but assimilates whatever
there is of good in such boundaries as it reaches out to a
fallen and falling world. Perhaps it would be more accurate

to say that the Church includes all national, temporal, and cultural boundaries.

Christianity reconnects us to universal history and by doing so provides a way for each human group, tribe, or nation to transcend its partial, sordid, and sinful past and be rescued from its limits and its wrongs. By his conversion savage man, for instance, reacquires a full human history, which in reality is his true history and true identity, and thereby begins to live his authentic life. Christ offers him the gift of eternal life, but it begins with the earthly gift of himself restored to plenary status within the universal human family.

But this is true not only for savage man; with our conversion we also begin the recovery of our full humanity, which makes us heirs to all human history and its eternal destiny. St. Paul says that in God we live and move and have our being. This means that only through a paradoxical surrender of our life to God do we experience the greater paradox of regaining the life that was so tragically diminished when sin entered the world.

But what does it mean specifically to regain the fullness of human life and history? As I ponder the question I realize I have understated our case. It is tempting to say the obvious: that through its peculiar custody of human history the Christian Church reestablishes and restores the reasonable, understandable plot of history and the destiny of mankind. The absurdity that Modern Enlightenment found in human history we now see as the absurdity of the Modern Age and another sad example of human hubris and poverty of understanding.

All this is certainly true, but there is more. Within the custodial care of the Church a new dimension reappears in history. It unfolds not only in temporal sequence-generations, geography, and time, as we have seen-but also in vertical, transcendent dimensions as well. As Pope John Paul II reminds us in *Memory and Identity*, God writes history with us, which means that it can never be mere and ordinary but presupposes always mankind's extraordinary destiny preordained in Genesis, fulfilled in Christ, unfolded in time, and consummated in eternity.

In an earlier chapter I introduced Miguel de Unamuno's notion of intra-history, that is, the intimate, unbroken, day-to-day march of history across the ages. It bears repeating that to some degree it is a vindication of woman's role in human history and in this way resembles the custodial view of the Church, which like Mary keeps the story of her children in her heart. In the eyes of God we never grow old and for this reason we remain children also to the Church despite all our wrongdoing and hardness of heart.

Yet without the transcendent good of the resurrected Christ working its way plot-like through history to justify and redeem it, intra-history makes no more sense than the godless versions of modern post-Enlightenment historians. Without the justifying goodness and purpose that Christ reasserted in human history it is as pointless at the humblest level as it is futile at the most universal.

We are nearing a final synthesis. I said earlier that the future is always the last dimension of history, but now it is necessary to add, for so we believe as Christians, that in a summary way of speaking God is the ultimate dimension of the future. I also said that because it exceeds the reach of rationalism history constitutes a superior form of reason inherent in human life. Now we can bring all these propositions together in a higher understanding by declaring that the reason of history, the reason that is human life acting in time, has a divine source. It is Christ who gives history and human life its meaning and purpose and by doing so makes it reasonable and enlightening. And by its light, shining on us since Eden, we are enabled to understand our life, knowing good from evil. In its final reach, therefore, we are bold to believe that the reason of history is the reason of God. From a Christian perspective this is a mystery of divine goodness, not a mere enigma shrouded in darkness but a mystery that is also an illumination to light our way to God and to signal his approach to us.

This is a delightful thought but it comes as no surprise to

believers, for Christianity has always taught us that illumination, intelligence, and every good gift come into this world from God.

✝✝✝

## 42. Christianity and the Fate of Religion

Many Christians see all the attacks on Christianity described earlier as nothing less than a satanic assault on the true religion and take them to be an obverse justification of the righteousness of their faith. Ultimately they are probably right, but without impugning their interpretation we can view these same phenomena from a more immediate historical perspective.

Given its universality and contributions to ethics, education, governance, art, law, and philosophy, Christianity not only has to its credit by far the greatest accumulation of earthly achievements of any religion but also makes the boldest claims in its theology. The founders of other religions were perhaps favored with divine revelations, which we may ponder and appreciate from a human perspective without compulsion of conversion. For even if we concede that they were enlightened, they were after all only enlightened men.

On the other hand, the claims made by and about Yeshua ben Miriam, or Jesus, son of Mary, are of a much greater order of magnitude and immediately thrust three choices before us: either he was who he claimed to be, or he was a deluded madman, or a clever charlatan. Accordingly, he either deserves our loyalty, our pity, or our contempt. There is no middle ground, certainly not the benign notion that Jesus was merely an interesting ethical teacher. Conventional human ethics is too narrow to accommodate what he taught. Yet if mad, no madman ever did the things he did; if a charlatan, no one has exposed his trickery or found his mortal remains; and if merely sane, no sane man ever said the things he said. This is why no other religious prophet or teacher arouses so much awe and animosity and why Christianity is at once the most majestic of religions and the most reviled.

In any case, Christian or not, much of the world marches in step with—or in conscious opposition to—the moral cadence of Christianity. And opposition is a form of acknowledgment. Whether or not its teachings have the additional virtue of being true is a matter that for the moment we shall leave intact.

Beyond the abolition of Christianity we glimpse the further aim of its adversaries: the eradication of the religious dimension of life. This is the explanation for the extraordinary assaults on Christianity, far greater than attacks on other religions. And here is the reason: if the anti-religious forces can demolish the Christian faith with all its theological depth and historical complexity and its enormous presence in the world, then it is unlikely that other religions can long survive in their present forms. The world would then be rid not only of Christianity but all other religions as well.

It is not generally understood how much other religions depend upon Christianity, how much its prestige stabilizes them in their claims to legitimacy and standing. Leading by example and tolerant for the reasons we have seen in its acknowledgements of other religions, Christianity provides a foundation from which these faiths make similar claims. Without Christianity very likely they would not rush triumphant into the vacuum as they might think, but would either vanish altogether or sink to the level of antiquated local superstitions.

The enemies of religion believe that once freed from the age-old dominion by priests, preachers, and prophets humanity would then pass into a more advanced historical phase, as philosophers Auguste Comte and Karl Marx offered as a hypothesis in the nineteenth century and which avid proponents argue as a conviction today. The question is whether it is possible to live humanly without a religious dimension in our life. Is God a vestige of our superstitious past, a name to cover our ignorance and answer to our fears, as the enemies of religion think, or are we constituted in such a way, as Saint Augustine and Pascal argued, that a God-shaped void at the center of our being will cause us always to yearn for the Divine?

✝✝✝

## 43. The Age of the Second Vision

In our day it seems that we have all become expert at speaking ill of the world, for we think it has failed our expectations and defrauded our hopes. And the disappointment hurts all the more because those hopes were placed so high. Thereby hangs a long historical tale. Most of it has been told in the preceding chapters. Here as we near the end of this book I shall summarize it and add some pertinent details.

Earlier I recounted how twenty-five centuries ago Classical Greek thinkers had come to see that man is someone—man or woman—who lives in a body and understands the world with reason and language. They celebrated human freedom, and in consequence of his freedom the Greek thinkers taught that man is responsible or irresponsible, good or bad, happy or unhappy, and, as Plato said, contemplates the exhilarating possibility of immortality.

Aristotle said that man chooses his life as the bowman selects his target. But what Aristotle did not say, because he did not see, was the Christian teaching that life also chooses man. If man aspires intellectually to reach God and immortality, as the Greeks taught, God also reaches out to offer man a much more glorious destiny, as Christians believe. For we are gathered into his kingdom not as slaves, nor merely as free, thinking persons, but as his beloved and favored children to whom is promised the fullness of eternal life and love. In our Father's house we shall be fully ourselves and fully loved, knowing and known, understanding and understood. Furthermore, Jesus taught that our ascension to a higher, happier state begins in this world. In the Beatitudes he said "blessed are," not "blessed will be." And the everlasting life grows stronger as earthly life falters along its mortal course. As believers we know that even as our mortal body declines our immortal life grows stronger. In the midst of life we are in death, wrote the Apostle Paul, but in the midst of dying we have already begun to live the undying life.

For many centuries this exalted Christian vision of life held, serving as a reservoir of inspiration for art, music, learning, law, governance, and morality. But in time the Christian fervor cooled and the vision began to fade. To many it seemed too good to be true and too ancient to be possible. Jesus, it seemed, had tarried too long in returning to earth and his promise was overdue for fulfillment. Men sought a new vision of life, and it was not long in forming. It came in two forms.

The first was a dual renewal within Christianity itself. The sixteenth-century Protestant Reformers sought, along with other motives, to reshape Christianity from within, to renew the vision, to rid the faith of corruption, medieval accretions and errors and rearm it with evangelical fervor.

Not to be outdone by the Protestants, in a counter reform the Catholic theologians determined to reenergize the Christian understanding from within the original Church. Organized shortly before the Council of Trent, the Jesuit order founded by St. Ignatius de Loyola emerged as the shock troops and the most energetic evangelical and teaching wing of Catholicism in the later decades of the sixteenth century. The Catholic Church lost most of Northern Europe to Protestantism but it converted whole nations beyond the seas and in the end emerged if not stronger at least more geographically extensive and demographically diverse than before. On a smaller but still impressive scale

Protestantism enjoyed a similar expansion.

But around the beginning of the seventeenth century both Catholic and Protestant versions of the Christian vision started to lose ground to an aggressive secular understanding of humanity. Kepler's *Astronomia nova vel Physica caelestis* (New Astronomy or Celestial Physics), 1609; Bacon's *Novem organum* (New Method), 1620; Galileo's *Dialogo dei massimi sistemi* (Dialogue on the Maximum Systems), 1632; and Descartes's *Discours de la méthode* (Discourse on Method), 1637 mark the initial phase of *La Nuova Scienza*, the "New Science." Not that the new age was limited to physical science and philosophy as we understand them today. It included the science of statecraft as Machiavelli's *Il Principe* (The Prince), circulated after 1515, and Huig de Groot's *De jure belli ac pacis* (On the Law of War and Peace), 1625 illustrate. At no certain, single date these works herald the start of a new age, the Modern Age from which only now we are beginning to emerge. Here I call it the Age of the Second Vision.

I indicated earlier that we have an intellectual and moral obligation to understand as far and as fairly as possible the interpretations that we ourselves may reject. We must ask, therefore, why many of the leading minds of the Modern Age abandoned the Christian understanding and preferred another interpretation, which from our vantage now seems inferior and unsatisfactory.

It will not do in the majority of cases to impute to the modern thinkers and discoverers unsavory, evil, or unethical motives. Perhaps they were beguiled by Descartes' Evil Deceiver, but if so they were not willing accomplices in the deception and in any case were no more or less susceptible to wickedness than we are. Every genuine thinker is sincerely convinced that he thinks the truth and, more, that it is his moral duty to make the truth known. We may disagree with the major propositions put forth by a Schopenhauer, or a Hegel, or a Heidegger, but it would be wrong of us to deny their sincerity, even when, to our way of thinking, they were sincerely wrong in several matters.

What we reject as errors in our day they earnestly expounded as truths in theirs. This admission is a somber warning not to rely too heavily on our own human understanding but always to measure it by the standards of revealed truth. Today's human truth has a disturbing tendency to become tomorrow's trash.

Among the many profound changes associated with the rise of the Modern Age two deserve our especial attention here. First, the Christian schism weakened the foundational Christian beliefs. Strangely enough, however, the decline was not readily apparent, and, in fact, on the surface the contrary seemed to be true. Religious debates, controversies, inquisitions, executions, and finally wars were violent signs of the times. But even though religious ideas and opinions abounded, or perhaps because they abounded, religious beliefs themselves became questionable, changeable, and most of all visible for all to see, debate, defend, and reject. As we saw in an earlier chapter, only when they begin to weaken and float to the surface do our normally oceanic beliefs become noticeable and therefore vulnerable. To debate a belief is probably a sign that it is in a declining, perhaps terminal phase.

At the same time Christianity converged with other forces: secular nationalisms, especially the pan-Germanism of Northern Europe, skeptical humanism in the style of Montaigne, and dynastic and colonial ambitions. The same Christian faith that once had united Europeans now divided them. For the first time, but far from the last, the worship of God carried with it a pledge of allegiance to king and country.

The rise of the vernacular languages posed a particularly vexing problem for Christian unity. Within their respective political and linguistic boundaries both English and German versions of the Bible led to an intensely nationalistic and personal identification with the Christian faith. The general spread of literacy, which occurred just as the national languages were maturing and the printing press was invented, meant that not only people (primarily men) could read for the first time but they could do so in their own tongues. As an additional noteworthy feature, the extraordinarily high literary level of the new German and English translations of the Bible not only quickly transformed them into classic literary treasures but soon stabilized and enriched their respective languages.

A very different situation developed in those lands where the Romance or neo-Latin languages prevailed. For them Latin was not, as it was for Northern Europeans, a wholly foreign language. The similarities between the offspring Romance tongues and their mother language caused Latin to be if not transparent at least what one writer called "translucent" to most Southern Europeans. For this reason— among others—there was no urgency to translate the Bible, which explains why it never became the classic standard of literary excellence in Catholic lands. For Catholic believers the Bible was untouchable, and this meant that it was not to be imitated in secular writing.

The new translations of the Bible in the Germanic areas of Europe, primarily England and the German kingdoms, led to contradictory results. There is no question that a great wave of Bible-based piety and evangelical fervor was fueled by the vernacular Scriptures. On the other hand, this same linguistic accessibility widened the chasm between Germanic-speaking Protestants and Latin Catholics. Literally and figuratively, they no longer spoke the same language. The thousand-year unity of Christianity was broken along yet another fault line.

Let us return now to the theme of Machiavellianism introduced briefly in an earlier chapter. The most notable early effect of the Machiavellian philosophy was a deep division between statecraft and morality. As Jacques Maritain points out, there arose as a consequence a false but deadly opposition between idealism, especially in an ethical sense, and what we would call today political or business reality. Of course princes and despots had been ruthless long before the time of Machiavelli, but *The Prince* not only gave them a rationale for being evil but a clear conscience to boot. In politics and later in business evil became good, and good, evil. The denial of ethics became the new ethics of the Modern Age. Indeed, ethics was adjudged to be evil if it stood in the way of political ambition.

From a Christian perspective, when State and politics are separated from the good by a reversal of classical ethics, they become the demonical realms and satanic strongholds about which the Apostle Paul wrote. And this principle applies as readily to democracies as to monarchies and other forms of government because, as we saw, it infected them all.

The problems of the Machiavellian vision of the world reduce to one: its eventual and utter failure. Throughout the Modern Age absolutist and democratic Machiavellians have succeeded and failed against other Machiavellians of similar stripe, but as Maritain says, they are merely dealing in counterfeit coinage. In politics and in commerce the Machiavellian is always ready for immediate success at the cost of eventual failure. And failure is assured because Machiavellianism corrupts the very substance and goodness on which it feeds, as rabies kills the dog and itself with its toxic infection.

We need go no further along these two dialectical pathways to make the argument. We have come far enough to see that when compared to the Machiavellian antagonisms in both wings of Western Christianity—for both Catholics and Protestants proved to be vulnerable to the Machiavellian machinations—and the corruption of the new nationalistic governments, science seemed to be the untainted way for free men to live the life of the mind, particularly in view of the new discoveries by scientifically rational men such as Galileo, Kepler, Descartes, and Harvey.

Under these circumstances the new or renewed reality of science appealed by virtue of its neat, unbiased methodology, its accessibility, and its dispassionate detachment from the sordid political and religious squabbles of the age. Its rules, which were simple, straightforward, and understandable, operated outside the heated polemics of the time.

Science became what Christianity had once been: a model of pure faith that served all men of honesty, dedication, and good will. It transcended national boundaries, languages, and cultures and at first seemed immune to Machiavellian ethical inversions. Meanwhile, in Protestant realms and to a lesser degree in Catholic lands, Christianity had molded itself in the images of diverse nationalisms.

But the Machiavellian spirit of modernity would not leave any good thing intact and untainted for long. Since it was based on astuteness, it soon learned to manipulate science for its own ends. As early as Leonardo da Vinci, scientists began designing instruments of war. By the time of Hitler scientific impartiality had become ethical indifference, and under the communists, political conformity.

Furthermore, as science indulged the modern Machiavellian State, scientists and philosophers distanced themselves from Christianity. The unhappy affair with Galileo— arguably more the fault of Galileo than the Church—had left a residue of suspicion and distrust in the intellectual world which worsened over the centuries into open hostility.

As the Modern Age ran its course, it gained the world and lost its soul. Philosopher George Santayana wrote that there was no hope for birth or death, save to enjoy the interval, and Ludwig Wittgenstein recommended that for want of certifiable truth to tell, philosophers ought to say nothing at all. Not that the Machiavellian spirit took the advice. The lack of truth became a license to rant, and persuasion won the day over ethics. A consensus of happy hypocrisy prevailed, an invincible knowledge of how not to be good, not to care, not to respect anything but power and the means of achieving it. But the difference is that today it has worked its way down from government to individual life. Machiavelli has become everyman.

Behind Machiavellianism in all its forms—political, religious, commercial—looms the spirit that feeds it: the assumption, spoken or otherwise, that there is no punishment for wrongdoing, which means ultimately there is no punisher of evil, in a word, no Creator, at least not one who minds the universe he has created.

I have painted a bleak picture of Machiavellian modernity. But not everyone subscribes to its code. Biologist LeConte du Nouy's book *Human Destiny* is the noblest version I have read of a refined humanism without God and personal immortality but also without Machiavelli. Written from a lofty perspective and in moving language, filled with sympathy for the human condition, in the briefest of declarations LeConte du Nouy rejects individual immortality and emphasizes instead the immortality of the human species. Like bees in a hive, individuals will die, but because of their efforts and sacrifices the hive will go on, just as we shall die utterly but the human race will go on to a better future and loftier achievements. Viewed from a Christian perspective, it is a book of infinite melancholy, a world away from "the peace that passes all understanding," far from the gaiety of the first Enlightenment Christian bashers, but with the somberness of later anti-Christian attitudes that came to dominate that era. Filled with pathos, awash with a sense of charity and sorrow, and permeated with a love of humanity, it comes close to the spirit of a mundane Christianity and a lesser Jesus who feels our pain and teaches brotherly love and solidarity—and gently tells us that we must reconcile ourselves to the end of our small life and that we can expect nothing beyond our mortality. Our consolation lies in the assurance that our race will go on as a collective immortality. Du Nouy's work could serve as a fitting epitaph for an age that promised men the world and gave them exactly that—and no more.

✝✝✝

## 44. The Living Perspective

The Bible begins from God's cosmic perspective which features man, his creation, fall, and redemptive destiny,

THE LIGHT OF EDEN

whereas most versions of philosophy start from the limited rationality of mankind and ideally, but not always, work their way toward the Divine, or in modern times, atheistically towards a void left by the non-existent Divine. This intellectual trajectory stands as the most remarkable, if not the greatest, achievement of Greek philosophy. In a magnificent tour de force the Greek thinkers reasoned their way out of and beyond polytheism and conceived the idea of God and immortality.

But we must be guarded in our praise of their feat. The idea of God—in Plato, for example—is still far from the revealed God of the Scriptures, much less the loving Father that Jesus taught, but it was the best unaided human intellect could do, and it was no small thing. But neither Greek thought nor its main philosophical derivatives—subjectivism (idealism) and objectivism (realism)—are much help against the relativism that dominates our time.

Yet it may be that we can commence to surpass modern relativism by considering our earthly life from a different perspective. If one wall of Jericho will not fall, then let us circle to trumpet from another side.

It is true that we live in a virtually limitless physical universe. We have heard them repeated so often that we are jaded by its unimaginable dimensions. But if we think about it, in a certain sense the universe is also encompassed within my life, else I could not encounter it and feel intimidated by its enormity at all. For I do not merely exist in the universe but rather live in it, and this is the key to everything I shall go on to say. Perhaps I am not apparent to the galaxy Andromeda, but Andromeda is apparent to me. This is not, as we usually suppose, a matter of disproportionate size but of different realities. Things appear within my life, but we have no reason to suppose that my life appears within lifeless things like galaxies and stardust. Our relationship is real and reciprocal but not a reciprocity among equals, for the advantage is mine, the higher reality of human life over matter.

For reality to appear to me at all, it must appear as a func-

*VII / A Christian Worldview* 173

tion of my life, as I live. Everything known and knowable, discovered and discoverable, possible and impossible, appears embedded in a precise personal, temporal, and historical way in "my life." Even those realities that transcend or overreach my life—God, for instance—also appear within my life. This can be taken to mean that my perception of the universe is also its quickening, or enlivenment. But this immediately calls for clarification.

Depending on its level of authenticity, living is what I do, freely and responsibly, or inertly and irresponsibly, and what happens to me as I do. As Christians we take the highest level of freedom and responsibility to be the Christian life, a level of life that is primarily biographical, nominative, and personal rather than merely biological, anonymous, and impersonal. God calls us by a personal name, not by kind, or characteristics, or species.

Since living is characterized by freedom and therefore is subject to choice and selectivity and to varying levels of authenticity, then it includes not only what we do but also what we could have done. Behind or alongside the choices we have made trail the aborted options, the phantoms of bypassed possibilities we could have chosen. Life is not a singular event but a constellation of real and rejected lives. This is one reason why human life cannot be reduced to a definition in the scientific manner; instead, as I argue here and later, human life reveals itself in a narrative mode. It is a story. But a story about what? About what I do, or did, or could do, or could have done, with things and with others. By my selections and rejections I coax things into releasing, or manifesting, their virtues and inconveniences, and in so doing I allow them to become my resources or my obstacles. One of the great myths and anxieties of modern times is that our resources are limited and that we may squander them. It is possible, of course, but only if first we exhaust our creative powers. For it is not resources that make man, but man who makes his resources.

In everyday life we say that "life goes on," and the truth goes much further than our platitude first suggests. Life is characterized by its "ongoingness" and cannot be otherwise. It is not a deed but a doing, not a fact but a gerund. Life, therefore, is not simply being, or a metaphysics of being, or a species of rationality, as older varieties of philosophy taught, but a coming into being, a becoming, an arriving, and a passing away. And at its deepest level, the historical level, this means that life reveals a moral and reasonable structure. In every phase and at each step, life is primarily the urgent task of making sense—and nonsense—of things, of separating the good from the bad, the wheat from the chaff, the workable from the unworkable, the desirable from the undesirable. Because of its urgency this imperative puts into play the totality of life. Rather than being confined to, or defined by, rationality alone, human life is reasonable in a much wider sense, for rationality is but a part, or degree, of the all-encompassing reasonableness that we call history. We could say, therefore, that life is reason, but it would more descriptive to say that living is reason in action over time. And because life is the task of making sense of the world, then it is understandable. If life were really absurd, meaningless, and formless, as modern writers like Camus and Robbe-Grillet claim, then we could not understand it at all, not even as a pointless absurdity. All literature presupposes the "sympathy of circumstances" described earlier.

Let us return now to the point offered earlier, namely, that insofar as it is perceptible everything must to some degree partake of and conform to my life. This means that the created world I perceive also becomes a component or filament in my story. Said in another way, it is enlivened insofar as I perceive it as my circumstance. To put it as a phenomenological principle somewhat compatible with modern thought, my life, and the life of each person, is the organizing, structural principle of reality, for everything appears within it circumstantially, that is, spatially and temporally. Nearness and farness, above and below, front and rear, surface and depth, here and there, then and now, great and small, are referential functions of my life and my perspective. These are some of the conditions under which I allow reality to manifest itself in my life.

Here we must be careful not to repeat a frequent mistake of modern philosophers and writers by thinking of "my" life as a solitary reality cut off from all others and incapable of communication, as existentialist writer Ernesto Sábato urges us to do in his novel *El túnel* (The Tunnel). Shall we forget so easily that no one comes into the world alone and that we all had mothers and probably families to boot? In fact, I could not think of my so-called solitary life as "mine" were there not other lives that are not "mine" to set it in defining apposition. Solitude is an obverse acknowledgement of others, just as ownership is defined by what we do not own. Life is inherently social and never more so than when we are anti-social and alone.

The modern thinkers tried to surpass the limits of human perspective by suppressing it. In so doing they converted modern thought into a sort of "out-of-the-body" exercise. Now after the experience of modern objectivity and its limitations, it appears to be time to reclaim intellectually our bodily life, to take up our place, and time, and circumstance, and rather than apologize for our human condition as though it were something unworthy of enlightened minds, to acknowledge that personal perspective is not only valid but the necessary condition for the manifestation of reality.

Our very condition is our proof: it is as though we were made for this world and this world made for us. It is as though the Judeo-Christian story of the creation were true. For contrary to what we have been taught in modern times, this humanized, quickened, circumstantial point of view is the only authentic standpoint from which to interpret and understand all reality. I repeat, the false perspective is reality seen "objectively," that is, from nowhere and by nobody.

Let us, therefore, draw a conclusion from what our experience and the Christian faith implicitly teach: the true perspective of the universe is a living, personal perspective. But this should come as no surprise to the believer. If God made mankind responsible for the world, then it makes sense that he also made the world in such a way that it would be responsive to mankind.

Consider Adam in the Garden. He was not haled as an equal or an inferior before things for their disposal. Nor was he, as the moderns thought, merely assigned a place as another thing or animal amongst the things and animals of Eden. Instead God brought the things and creatures of Eden before Adam and placed them under his watch and dominion. By divine consent and approval Adam humanized the Garden and converted it into his circumstance, that is, a livable world. In this sense, we all reenact the drama of Adam, for we, too, must personalize the world and make it ours. After all, according to the Bible, this susceptibility to human life was what the world was all about from the beginning.

Here, however, three cautions are in order before we get carried away by our dialectic: first, "enlivenment" does not mean "alive" or "living." By perceiving it I do not create a sentient universe, that is, I do not cause things to come to life, but to come to and through my life in order to be perceived. Second, I do not project things from my mind or consciousness, as Fichte and other great German idealists taught. Things are what they are, or can be, but *with me*, and I am who I am, or can be, but *with them*. God created us for a world, specifically this world, and he created the world for us, concretely for me, that "me" that is each person born into the world. It makes no more sense to speak of things in themselves than it does to try to think of myself as a solitary being without them. With me things are released within the limits of my life and my perspective to be what they are. They need me in order to be themselves, and I need them in order to become who I am. By releasing them to be what they are, I also convert them into the resources for forging my life, for doing the things I must do in order to go on living. This is encapsulated in Ortega y Gasset's celebrated saying: "I am I and my circumstance, and if I do not save it, I do not save myself." From this understanding of my relationship to things, and theirs to me, the otherwise baffling and mysterious passages in *Romans* (8:19-22) can take on different and deeper meanings, human meanings, for the world and I appear bound to each other in intimate, reciprocal dependency. Third, my perspective of reality does not exhaust reality. The world is more than we know and more than we see. Yet what I see is worthy, for what I see no one else can see in exactly the same way. But by that same reasoning, what I cannot perceive in things others can. Poetry and art are the immediate proof. Each of us bears a responsibility to creation and a duty to blend our partial vision with the infinite perspective. For we have reason to believe that our portion of truth is also truth to God.

This means that the material, social, and historical universe, which presses in on me and was here before me and may be here long after I am gone, appears within my life—and only within my life—and we can reasonably say, within the life of every person as well. This is a mystery; the world that was and the world to be, the time that was and the time to come, are also a comprehended part of my life and time here and now.

There is more. My life, in which I have my physical being, cannot be reduced to my mortal body. My life is where and how I encounter all reality and where and how reality encounters me. This includes not only the entirety of perceivable things, transcendent realities, possibilities, and impossibilities, but also—and primarily—the physical person that I am. And if this is true, then my life cannot be merely another thing in the parade of manifested realities, as the modern materialists teach; that is, my life cannot be both the stage on which realities make their appearance and one of the realities themselves. It cannot be both stage and actor. For even though in a commonsense view that I in no way dispute, the world preceded me, that temporal precedence itself, along with all other knowable features and realities reemerges through my life as my enlivened circumstance. Everything I know or experience becomes knowable and experiential within my life. My life encompasses and thus arranges all creation—past, present, and future—into my enlivened, personalized circumstance. In this way all history becomes my history; the entire past, my past; the future, my future; and the world, my world.

With these intriguing possibilities in mind, we return to the perplexity that has humiliated modern mankind. Where do I—and everyone else—stand to perceive the universe and all that is contained in it, including the divine realities that reach beyond it? Are we banished to the far side of the cosmos away from the bright center of creation? No. We are here, of course, as always in the center of our circumstance in an enlivened, reciprocal relationship with all perceived reality. Since Eden the mission of mankind has been to convert reality near and far into a humanized "world." The world and I need each other, and God has, or so it seems, so marvelously made the universe that each person lives at the center of creation, else reality could not be my circumstance, *circum + stantia*, that which "stands around" me. Gray was wrong in his beautiful elegy. No flower is born to blush unseen but instead flourishes at the center of creation. In like manner, none of us is out of God's direct light and vision. In a sense deeper than modern science and philosophy have understood, or can admit, *the Christian vision of the world was true.* Except that the center is infinitely greater than early Christians knew. Indeed, without intending to, modern science has vindicated the older understanding. In this marvelously crafted universe where every person mysteriously resides at the center, the sun still rises and sets to our east and west, worlds rotate around us, the stars still shine down on us, and the cosmos keeps its place in vast symmetry around our central place in this central world.

Before leaving the topic let me respond to an oblique objection certain to be raised to what I have just written. Does this supposed vindication of the medieval ethos mean that we are in danger of returning to its archaic notions, for instance, a flat earth and quaint fears of falling over its edges? Not at all, because educated people in the Middle Ages never subscribed to the flat earth theory to start with. As for the uneducated, probably they were as victimized by ignorance and superstition in that age as they are in ours. Like the Classical Greek philosophers from whom they inherited the notion, medieval thinkers knew the earth was a sphere, and for their part, sailors always had a practical knowledge of the earth's curvature. St. Thomas Aquinas speaks of round worlds in his writings, and in *Le Livre du Trésor* (The Book of the Treasure), an encyclopedic compendium of knowledge published in a deliciously archaic French in 1284, Bruno Latini not only says the earth is round but also gives surprisingly accurate comparative sizes of the sun, earth, moon, and several of the planets. For his part, Marco Polo wrote that if one were to travel to the west and encountered no obstacles in the journey that eventually one would return from the east. Two and a half centuries later Christopher Columbus tried to prove him right and the Magellan/El Cano expedition actually did so.

If not from medieval culture, then where did the myth of the flat earth originate? From where we would least expect it. In his book *Inventing the Flat Earth: Columbus and the Historian*, Jeffrey B. Russell gives plausible evidence that the supposed belief in a flat earth was a post-Enlightenment fable created to discredit Christianity. It did not become fixed in the public mind until the late nineteenth century or early decades of the twentieth.

## 45. Mediating Mortality

But here mortality casts its shadow over all I have said about "my life." Does death render it empty and illusory? Intellectual honesty compels us to admit the possibility. We walk by the convictions of faith, not by the proofs of sight, yet at the same time we are not blind to the evidence of our eyes. To our chagrin we die, and to our sorrow so do all those we cherish. And in those fateful moments the commonsense world puts our faith to the test with its skepticism and demands of proof for our hope. How do we respond?

Among the many features that appear in my life I discover my own mortality. *Mors certa, hora incerta* (Certain death, at an uncertain hour) said the ancients. This random inevitability—if I may use such a term—is and has been understood in two ways. To the non-believer death means simply the annihilation of the person and the end of the story.

For the Christian believers (and several other religions), on the other hand, even though their life contains death as an inevitable certainty, they advance the argument that life must be greater than death in order to contain it, as the larger contains the smaller. The dialectical paradigm is this: death happens but life contains it, survives it, surpasses it, and goes on. To the unbeliever, life is consumed by death; for the believer, death is swallowed up in life.

We must admit that the skeptical materialist is at least partially right. *What* I am—the object and the physicality of my life—is consigned to mortality, but *who* I am—the subject of my life—comprehends an eternal panorama. For I am not my body, at least not just my body; I did not choose it and may not even be pleased with it, and its death does not necessarily coincide with "my" death. The Bible tells us so. It may be, of course, that the biological death of my body causes my personal biographical death also, as the skeptics assert, but this remains to be seen—and proved. And the skeptics take on the burden of proof by their assertions. For I repeat: I am not my mortal body but someone who lives toward a future that in principle and perspective is virtually, eternally unlimited.

Why should it be so? Is it cruel or indifferent irony? Or do past, present, and future appear to me in my life because it is my destiny, and the destiny of each person, to possess the fullness of their eternal creation? No one can say for sure, but there is more reason to believe than cause to doubt.

Furthermore, in a paradoxical way that only faith can make any sense of, death itself must appear in and through my life—and thus be "enlivened" in order to be perceived at all. In other words, death becomes a circumstantial component of my life. Death is always with us, we die daily says St. Paul, but it is with us in life and as a part of life. Life, then, is the vantage point for contemplating death and placing it in perspective. In this sense death presupposes life and cannot be a reality apart from it. It is enveloped and swallowed up in life. This is simplistic, of course, and to put it even more simplistically, we live to die, as the unbeliever tells us, but we die in life, and as the believer goes on to declare, we die to live.

Here we come to a more mysterious question related to our theme. We have taken some time to point out the distances separating these realities: my physical being and "my life"—the life of each person. Now we ask why such a chasm exists between my life and my mortal being. Why should my life and I be in such a disproportionate relationship? Why is my life so much wider and greater than my physical being, the "I" understood as the subject of my life?

Who can say? We do know from the biblical account in *Genesis* that humanity fell from an original higher state. Is that fall reflected in the vast separation between the mortal man that I am and the unlimited dimensions of "my life?" If the rupture of the exalted human condition resulted from the fall in Eden, does our restoration come about by expanding the mortal person that I am to its original boundless, eternal condition? In short, am I destined to recover the fullness of my life and to rejoice in the restored fullness of all those I love? As it is, we are aware of being only partially and imperfectly ourselves in this life, but we know also even in our fallen condition that the better life consists of always becoming more than we are. If this is true, and true following our death, then we shall live again in the fullness of our personhood. We shall finally and eternally be the person we were created to be.

There is more: since life consists formally of always going on, and since for all its unthinkable differences and expansions my heavenly life will, in some fashion, still be *my* life, then it stands to reason that it will still be subject to becoming. If this is true, then can we not begin to think of heaven as dynamic movement from perfection to greater perfection, from happiness to greater happiness, from work to greater work? The Bible itself declares that we shall have responsibilities in keeping with our preparation in this life. In this sense Heaven would be becoming the persons God created us to be, levels of being we cannot begin to imagine in this limited life.

As Teilhard de Chardin taught so well in *The Divine Milieu*, this expectation is remote from all forms of pantheism. As Christians we do not contemplate the annihilation of our personhood in the ocean of Divine Sublimity. Quite the opposite, we look forward to the plenitude of the life that was prefigured by our Christian life in this world. Else we must wonder why God would bother with our creation at all. The Father does not reabsorb his children but delights in their growth, achievement, and maturity. This may be a simplistic understanding, but it is the way God has taught us to think about him.

† † †

## 46. The Non-Existent God

A great many people say that God does not exist. I agree with them, except that I would go further and argue that neither do people. But hear me out before rushing to judgment.

To begin with a preliminary step, it seems necessary to believe in God in a limited way before one can deny his reality. We do not have to deny the reality of unicorns because nobody believes in them. But in the case of God, we must first acknowledge that there is present a belief in God. To put it in simpler words, God is present as a belief and therefore as a reality of sorts, even if his reality is similar to that of a fictional character. Then it becomes a matter not of denying God directly but of skirmishing with the belief that some people have in him. God, therefore, is to the unbeliever a defective belief, that is, a belief without a justifying content, in short, an unjust belief, a belief that violates or deals unfairly with reality. This perspective accounts, I suppose, for the peculiar anger that unbelievers often demonstrate when the subject of God comes up.

But then conceding the belief itself, we proceed to the problem of the existence of God. Unamuno once said that God does not exist but instead "super-exists" (*sobreexiste*), and from his superior existence he sustains us in our existence. I applaud the courage of the great Basque thinker, for I think he was on track of an important truth, but I suggest that his terminology was deficient. I would say, as the Bible says, that instead of existing or super-existing in the mode of things, God *lives* as the Divine Person he is, the Living God, and because he lives, we also live, for we are created in his image and likeness.

If we unpack it for concealed significance, language itself gives us hints of the enormous distance between material existence and personal life. The Bible refers to God as the great I AM, and Jesus said to the Pharisees not "before Abraham was, I *exist*," but "I *am*," an intensely personal way of saying "I live." And he lives in a mysterious manner that annuls the confinements of temporality. Apparently Jesus breaks the rules of syntax because eternity supersedes the rules of time. Except for literary license or fictional personification, ordinary language does not permit material existence to speak in the first person; only persons, divine, angelic, and human have that privilege. And we have seen that "my life," the life of each person, is that strange, radical reality to which I must refer all other realities and, conversely, that insofar as they are perceivable all other realities, real, possible, or impossible, appear within and through it. Modifying Unamuno's celebrated insight, perhaps we could say of God that He "super-lives," and out of his superior, overflowing life and love he sustains and renews us in our life.

But does it really matter which words we choose to describe life? Indeed, it matters and matters greatly. Had our thinkers clearly understood the difference between existence and human life, perhaps we would have been spared the bleak philosophies and dehumanized sciences of modern times which destroyed the eternal hopes of so many and deposited a spiritual poison in modern mankind that continues to sicken the soul. Yes, it matters.

† † †

## 47. The Christian Imperative

We looked earlier at things that went wrong in the modern world, what I have called the Age of the Second Vision. Yet it would intellectually immoral to leave matters there and offer no alternatives to it. And here this book reaches its most delicate stage. As I said earlier, we have all become experts at carping, but after the complaining the question then becomes, do we have anything better in mind, or are we capable only of accusations? When words are salt in the wound, silence is balm.

As Christians it would be easy for us simply to say that we must return to Jesus and repeat with faithful but disloyal Peter that only Christ has the words of eternal life. But we cannot go back to where we have never been. The world, even the so-called Christian world, was never more than partially Christianized. If at first this seems like a harsh indictment of two thousand years of Christianity, it is more a hope for the future ages of mankind to come in this world. If the Christian vision failed it was because Christians failed the vision. But this means the vision and all the richness it implies is intact and waiting for us to claim it.

In any event, we cannot be Christians of the past. It is a cliché, but a cliché of the truth, to say there is never any going back in history or in life. God is not a God of the past, the past that passed away with dead history; he is not the God of the dead but of the living. When we try to return to the past we always end up in counterfeit country. Instead we must go forward to Christianity. The Christian imperative of our time is not merely to hold to the faith of our fathers but also to live the faith and prepare the future of our children and grandchildren and the generations that may follow them. This is not a pious play on words. Our forefathers kept the faith—even if they did not always live it—but we must do more than keep it. It is our task and our privilege to fulfill the faith, to live it to the full. How? Let us collect the questions, reserving the option of returning to them later.

At the same time this does not mean that we are to be indifferent to the Christian past or that our Christianity is merely a faith for the third millennium, as though we were beginning anew without lingering debts or dues. Christianity is old and cannot ignore its age without a measure of falsification. We are fond, perhaps too fond, of neat, numerical restarts and live under many numerological fixations that weigh unduly on our life. Of course with Christ we can begin anew, but our renewal, our rebirth is the renewal of all that was true, and good, and worthy before. What we do for Christianity as Christians in our time, what we believe, preserve, discover, develop, or improve, we do also for the Christians of earlier times, for all those who make up the "cloud of witnesses" of which Paul speaks. We enhance or deplete the past—which was somebody's present—by how we live today. We are the future of the past, its last dimension, its present hope for a just and honorable completion. Like the classic Chinese custom according to which a descendant who rose to higher estate elevated his ancestors in honor, so to honor Christ in our time is to honor Christians in all times. This is a further dimension of what some churches wisely call the "communion of saints."

We have the obligation to pray daily, as Jesus taught us, first that the Father's Name be hallowed, then in immediate sequence for the coming of his Kingdom, and finally in petition for our physical needs, for reciprocal forgiveness of sins, and for protection from the Wicked One.

The Lord's Prayer is starkly yet brilliantly simple and serves as a universal bond among all Christians, yet it contains a reference to perhaps the ultimate Christian mystery, what the Bible calls the Kingdom of God. Of this Kingdom I know very little and thus can have little to say, but I do know that Jesus spoke of it more than anything else. It is the gist of nearly all his parables and the ultimate horizon of his teaching. Late in his public ministry he also spoke, somewhat abruptly in the biblical context, of his intention to establish his Church, his *Ekklesia*, that is, "the ones called out." Called out of what and for what purpose? Surely it referred to persons called out of the sinful world and made ready to live in his Kingdom. The Church is not the Kingdom itself but an indispensable pre-figuration of the Kingdom.

Generally speaking, we Christians have understood Christianity to mean both an insurance against the fires of Hell and an assurance of our everlasting life in Heaven. But what shall we say about the world we leave behind at death? Does our responsibility lapse with our mortality? Surely not; Christ himself never intended to abandon the world and let it sink to utter dereliction. He came into the world to save his creation, and if he did so, then it must mean that the world is worth saving, as are we. In Eden God esteemed man enough to make him responsible for the whole world. As far as I know, that responsibility was never rescinded. It was our sin that brought ruin on the world, and it may be that in ways we do not fully understand it is our redemption that will restore it.

Periodically throughout their history Christians have tried to outdo one another in proclaiming their worthlessness. At times we would do well to remember without boasting that we are not worms and wretches but God's highest creation, bearing the very image and likeness of the Creator. Do we not risk dishonoring God when we belittle ourselves? Our human life is the most precious of creations and a cause for gratitude and thanksgiving, never a justification for self-loathing. We must love others and ourselves as God loves us. Nothing easier to preach, nothing harder to practice.

Christ founded his Church and declared that Hell would not prevail against it. I ask again, was he mistaken? We Christians have divided his body into countless branches. We cannot see the ecclesiastical forest for the trees and have all but lost sight of the united Church in a bewildering jungle of churches. We often celebrate the fact that most of our Christian denominations agree on the fundamentals of the Christian faith and form a common front on a wide range of social, moral, and even theological issues. But in reality our deep similarities are themselves an indictment and our secondary divisions a permanent scandal. Christ established one Church; our forefathers gave us thousands more. In democratic, freedom-loving lands we had the freedom to divide, never the divine or scriptural permission to do so, at least none that I know of.

Do not all Christians, including Catholics, stand accused by the ecclesial multiplicity of the Modern Age? Only if we are confirmed neo-Platonists can we think of the unity of the Church in purely ethereal or mystical terms. Church unity was surely meant to be physical and creedal, just as the Kingdom was clearly to include an earthly dimension. Else why would St. Paul and the other New Testament writers have emphasized unity so much and opposed schism and heresy so forcefully? Aside from the four Gospels most of the remainder of the New Testament is a series of apostolic or early post-apostolic letters exhorting the congregations and warning against heresies, false teachers, and deviations from the apostolic teachings.

I raise these questions only to make this point: as Christians are we not clearly under an urgent ecumenical injunction? I do not know how or when the Kingdom of God will come into manifest reality, and as far as I know nobody does, but it stands to reason that our internal disunity and discord hinder its coming. We pray every day for the Kingdom to come, and then do we not go indifferently on our divided Christian ways? Have we lived so many long years and centuries in disunity that we have lost sight of our disjunctive abnormality? It does no good to accuse the impassioned men of a former age of sowing disunity. What's done was done for the motives of that age. But we have no cause to continue in their mistakes and recommit their sins. We were called to be Christians as persons and as a people, and the two dimensions are inseparable. Can we reasonably deny that the first mandate of today's Christians must be a wholehearted movement towards unification of the Christian world? It sounds impossible, but nothing is more impossible than what we are unwilling to try, no battle more lost than the one we refuse to fight. If the Church is the Body of Christ, as we say, then how can we tolerate the tragedy of a dismembered Christ? How long shall we so cavalierly and tolerantly continue his further crucifixion? Christians of the world, unite!

We have spoken about the deficiencies of Machiavellianism, philosophic minimalism, biological reductionism, and other intellectual creations of the Modern Age. Now, we must ask in the same critical attitude, what alternatives have we as Christians to counter and replace them? We subdue a false idea only with a true one. It does little good to establish Christian schools and universities if we teach the same theories as the secular world, or worse, if our Christianity consists merely of opposing modernity. For that would mean that we are intellectually dependent on what we oppose, mere parasites clinging like fleas on a dog to the modern corpus of bogus knowledge.

As Christians we have a daunting intellectual imperative ahead of us: we must create new theories with a Christian foundation, theories deeply respectful of human life and deeply obedient to divine teachings. We need, among many other creations, a new anthropology, or theory of human life, a new aesthetics and a new understanding of art, a new philosophy and sociology of human and social reality, and real alternatives to the pervasive Machiavellian interpretations of statecraft, business, and human behavior. We must go beyond the likes of Machiavelli, Freud, Marx, Hawking, and others whose thought is recklessly at odds with God, to say nothing of faithless or feckless theologians of all denominations who from within gnaw at Christianity like termites. We cannot continue to concede the intellectual terrain to the secular mind—nor to divided and enfeebled Christian minds—and then expect to hold our ground, much less retake what we have lost over the course of the Modern Age.

Christian intellectual hesitancy is understandable. For centuries believers have feared that intellectual inquiry would veer towards heresy, yet they have lazily and paradoxically compromised with assorted second-rate ideologies and philosophies. A greater heresy has been our Christian mindlessness, our meek acceptance of dehumanizing theories, our readiness to accommodate, retreat, and tolerate. In *The Scandal of the Evangelical Mind*, Mark Noll describes how contemporary evangelical Christians have fallen into simplistic, regressive thinking. But as easily he could have spoken for a wider Christian spectrum. Aside from a small cadre of theologians and philosophers, low intellectual standards have become generalized in Christianity of all persuasions. The signs of the times tell us that the secular world is past the point of no return on its way to intellectual bankruptcy, yet we Christians have little intellectual capital available to rescue it. But we have the mind of Christ to guide us, and that advantage is all we need if we put our minds to it.

St. Augustine believed at one point in his life that as the failing Roman government slid into chaos the Church might have to assume political responsibility for Hippo and the surrounding province. It may come to that point for us again under conditions of political fragmentation unthinkable at the moment. For the world—Christian and pagan, democratic and dictatorial—is becoming ungovernable. The time may come when the Church will be the only remaining organized body capable of assuming responsibility for the fate of people. If it happened tomorrow, would the Church be ready? Or would our disunited churches vanish also in the general social and governmental collapse?

Pray that such a time never come. Nevertheless, another general Christian imperative remains intact: we must not only pray for the Kingdom to come and that God's will be done on earth as it is in Heaven but live and prepare as though it could come tomorrow. And when it does come, shall Christ find a community of squabbling dunces and lazy laborers? If so, we shall probably be rewarded accordingly, as the parable of the talents illustrates so starkly.

Persecuted early Christians often retired from the world, sequestering themselves in caves and dwelling in deserts. In his book *In the Heart of the Desert* John Chryssavgis provides a fascinating summary of the tradition of the Desert Fathers and Mothers that enriched the early Christian centuries. It is a mystery why the drier the land the richer spiritual life tends to be, indeed, why nearly all religions were born in deserts. Yet as fruitful as it was, the tradition of these Christians represented only one facet or possibility of Christianity. As it was, they left a lingering doubt in Christianity whether it was better to flee the world or minister to it. In any case, there remains a multitude of perspectives yet to be developed for the common and supernatural good of mankind. After two thousand years Christianity contains dimensions of truth that are virtually unexplored. Unknown plentitudes of knowledge and spiritual treasures, and immeasurable benefits for humanity, only await those with sufficient vision, generosity of spirit, and stoutness of mind to delve into its limitless reserves of truth and power.

There is an expectation, more stoic than Christian and exacerbated by Calvinist and Jansenist teachings in recent centuries, that we need not bother our heads with such mighty matters as I describe here. God will take care of things, we are told; he will unite his scattered Church and establish his Kingdom when he chooses, with or without our effort and cooperation. Of course he will, if he chooses; God is the master of all possibilities; yet he has a way, one could say a preference and a history, of working through people, even such unlikely people as we. But he does not reward confusion or sloth. Surely Christ alone could have wrought all the things he empowered his disciples to do. Obviously he had the power to do so himself if he could confer it on others. Yet he chose to work through them, and we can work assured that he chooses still to effect his purposes through us. The salvation of the world then becomes a corporate, cooperative venture between God and the faithful. In this sense we have the incredible privilege of enlisting in the building of the Kingdom, of being the hands of God, or to understand it in plainer terms, as field hands in the harvest. This is why it is not enough for us simply to go to church, we must be the Church; not enough for us merely to belong to a church, we must become the Church.

In this regard there is a startling yet hopeful dimension of the Qumran documents that may hold lessons for us today. The mysterious Essenes and similar communities about which we know little were united in the fervent belief that when they had been made ready by prayer, pure sinless living, and earnest expectation, the long-awaited Messiah would appear. And not only the Messiah himself but that in preparation for his coming the supernatural beings we call angels would descend to dwell among men. We do not know very much about the circumstances surrounding Jesus' life. But we know that indeed he appeared as though in response to these extraordinary preparations. Will he come again when we have been made ready by prayer, sinless living, and earnest expectation? And will he delay until we have been made ready?

I asked how to live by faith. Surely it is not a matter of giving an answer but in being an example. And just as surely it begins with the determination to rid our personal and public life of those things to which death or the return of Christ would be an embarrassment or an impediment. We must ask ourselves, therefore, which things really matter, really interest us, really are worth our while, things to which death itself is not an objection or a contradiction. For

THE LIGHT OF EDEN

me, if a thing, an act, or a course of behavior appears to interest me, but death would negate that interest, then it cannot truthfully be said that it is of enduring interest. Only those things that preserve their interest through and beyond death itself truly matter.

It is good to ponder the mighty works and grand sweep and scope of God's power and mercy. But there are moments when our soul turns as dry as desert sand, when what St. John of the Cross calls "the dark night of the soul" descends on us. What then?

Faith, hope, and love are called in some strains of Christianity the Theological Virtues. About them and always in their company hovers the general virtue of courage. When spiritual bleakness comes, as it surely comes to us all, and we can barely rise in the morning and dread to lie down at night, then we must summon the courage to persevere and to convert our very weakness to patience and strength. When faith, hope, and love will not sustain us, then we must sustain them. In the soul's dark night, amid the pain and the dread, we must keep a grip on basic certainties: speak the truth and we will become truthful; imitate virtue and we will become virtuous; practice hope and we will become hopeful; practice love and we will be loving; practice being who we should be and we will become who we are; resist the Devil and he will flee from us; seek the Lord and he will find us; cry out to him in the desert dryness and he will lead us to springs of living water; act like Christ and we will become Christ-like, a blessing to men and a pleasure to God.

I have raised questions and by implication left more unanswered. But as I said earlier in this book, genuine thought progresses not so much by the measure of its answers as by the meaningfulness of its questions. This has always been a mystery to philosophers themselves. But from the Christian perspective perhaps we can begin to see why it should be so. To ask the questions that are humanly perplexing is to be drawn ever further into the mysteries of creation and deeper into the brilliant wonders of God. The

*VII / A Christian Worldview* 193

general Scriptural principle holds true, and nowhere more than in the philosophical quest for truth: ask and ye shall receive, knock and it shall be opened to you. Some turn away from the enlightening search, as modern men have turned away to lesser answers, but for the Christian thinker the majesty of God and the mystery of human destiny converge in a metaphor of eternal revelatory light that illuminates our way even as it surges ahead of our understanding. This illumination is what I have been calling in this book *The Light of Eden*.

# EPILOGUE

I began this book many years ago as a recovering skeptic; I end it sustained by an unshakable truth: the lordship of Jesus Christ, who was crucified for our sins and rose from death that we might live eternally. Everything I have said and the Christian worldview I have tried to outline flow from this simplest of creeds, which is also the deepest of mysteries. If it is true, as philosopher Unamuno claimed, that every genuine book is a novel at some level, then this is the novel of my Christian journey. And I have far to go.

Every book, like every person, has a destiny, abortive, brief, or brilliant. Naturally I wish the best for my work, but regardless of its fate, for me it was time well spent and effort well rewarded. I set out to write a book for others but I reaped the first fruits of the experience. For that alone and above all else I am grateful and happy with the effort. It could have been better, as human things can always be better, but it was the best I could do with the talents I had. Not that I can boast of anything worthwhile it may contain. According to the popular Christian saying, we do our best and God will do the rest. I think we have it reversed: God does the best; it is we who do the rest—as best we can.

My hope for this book is that despite its imperfections and my shortcomings, it will let some of "the Light of Eden" shine through its pages to penetrate this present darkness, lighting our way, clearing our mind, and dispelling our fears as we incline in our existential hurt and longing to God and he inclines to us in his eternal mercy and love.